Road to Growth

How Lagging Economies
Become Prosperous

Fred McMahon

Atlantic Institute for Market Studies
Halifax, Nova Scotia
2000

Published by Atlantic Institute for Market Studies
1657 Barrington Street, Suite 521
Halifax NS B3J 2A1

Telephone: (902) 429-1143
Fax: (902) 425-1393
E-mail: aims@aims.ca
Web site: www.aims.ca

Canadian Cataloguing in Publication Data
Fred McMahon,

> Road to Growth

> Includes bibliograhpical references and index
> ISBN 1-896928-02-1

1. Economic development — Case studies. I. Atlantic Institute for Market Studies. II. Title.
HD87.M318 2000   338.9   C00-950005-7

Printed and bound in Canada
Second Printing, March 2000

Cover illustration: Edgar Beals
Page Layout: EE Editorial Services

Acknowledgements

A generous grant from the Donner Canadian Foundation made this work possible. I can only hope it matches in merit the many other contributions to public-policy debate across Canada that the foundation has supported.

I need to thank two AIMS presidents, Brian Lee Crowley and Don Cayo, whose patience was also required for the completion of the work. At almost every point in the process, I have been behind schedule, and they both cheerfully suffered through incessant delays.

Former Irish Prime Minister John Bruton generously contributed the insightful foreword. Mr. Bruton, of course, played a key role in Ireland's powerful economic growth in recent years. His words go well beyond the standard introductory piece and contribute genuine value to this volume.

Numerous people in the jurisdictions examined in this book were extremely generous with their time and insight in helping a stranger from far away try to understand what makes their economies tick.

The many advance reviewers of the book, particularly from the AIMS Board of Research Advisors, generously helped with insightful comments and strong criticism where I went wrong. Any remaining errors are my responsibility.

Elizabeth Eve has ably led the production team. Peter King has carefully copy-edited the book. And Edgar Beals provided the delightful cover illustration.

My mother, Phyllis McMahon, turned 80 just as this book entered into production. I would like to dedicate it to her.

Fred McMahon
Senior Policy Analyst
Atlantic Institute for Market Studies

Contents

Foreword

It is an honour to be invited to write a foreword to Fred McMahon's book *Road to Growth*. I was first introduced to Mr. McMahon, and to the Atlantic Institute for Market Studies, through the latter's web site.

I was preparing a speech for delivery in St. John's, Newfoundland, on the lessons that Atlantic Canada might draw from Ireland's recent economic success.

I have long been a regular visitor to Newfoundland, because southeastern Newfoundland is the most Irish place in the world outside Ireland itself, and an Irish visitor feels more at home there than anywhere else.

At the time, Mr. McMahon gave me a very clear insight into the factors that have prevented Atlantic Canada from achieving its full economic potential.

In Ireland's case, our full economic potential was not achieved for a long time. Generations of Irish people had to emigrate, never to return.

Between 1949 and 1989, it is estimated that 815,295 people emigrated from Ireland. This represents 22% of our current population. I understand that the equivalent emigration figure for Newfoundland over the same period would be about 25% of its current population.

Now, thanks to our success, instead of having to bid up wages to recruit staff, expanding firms in Ireland find that they can recruit among the Irish abroad. Descendants of earlier Irish emigrants also help us achieve a good audience in the boardrooms of multinational companies.

So the population loss of an earlier era has become a benefit in this era.

The challenge for Atlantic Canada is to create the conditions whereby it too can tap the talents and influence of Atlantic Canadians who have gone to live elsewhere.

Ireland and Atlantic Canada have had a common proclivity towards accumulating government debt. At one time, Ireland's debt reached 125% of our GDP, a debt of crisis proportions. It is now back down to about 60% of our GDP, thanks to the economic success described in Mr. McMahon's book.

The problem of Ireland's debt has had some beneficial side effects. In the 1970s, the initial borrowing enabled us to maintain social and educational infrastructure through the hard times of the oil crisis. It was a cushion against radical political upheaval at a time of a fall in real national income.

In the 1980s, the necessity of debt control meant that Ireland avoided some of the costly political errors of continental Europe. We did not undertake unrealistic pension commitments, or over-protect labour markets. The debt problem also brought about social partnership between employees, employers, and government in the late 1980s. This kept wage increases below productivity growth.

Both Ireland and Atlantic Canada have been recipients of transfers respectively from the European Union and Canada.

The motive for these transfers has been laudable in both cases – to narrow the gap in incomes between regions and to build political cohesion.

As Fred McMahon's book shows, there is a price to be paid for such largesse. The natural process of economic adjustment is postponed. Vested interests opposed to change are built up. This leads to a misallocation of resources.

In Ireland's case, the E.U.'s Common Agricultural Policy has maintained agricultural incomes and prices in Ireland at a far higher level than would have been possible using Irish taxpayer's money. But Irish agriculture is now less efficient than it was in 1972, when we joined the E.U., and this has happened because of E.U. subsidies.

Ireland does not participate in an E.U.-wide system of employment insurance, in the same way as Atlantic Canada participates in a Canadian E.I. system. If there had been a uniform rate of unemployment benefit for all of Europe, at rates that would be acceptable in (say) Germany, both minimum-wage rates and consequent unemployment in Ireland would undoubtedly have been much higher. This would probably have killed off the Celtic Tiger at birth.

There are many very valuable insights for policy-makers in Mr. McMahon's book. He makes the very important assertion that there is a natural rate at which economic growth will tend to raise the incomes of poorer regions towards those of richer regions. The "convergence theory" of Barro and Sala-i-Martin suggests that, each year, a lagging region closes the gap with a leading economy by between 2 per cent and 3 per cent, which implies that it would take about 25–35 years to close the gap by a half. This theory would suggest that, if politicians were to do nothing except let markets operate, the poorer will catch up with the richer over time.

McMahon's chapter on Ireland is, to my mind, comprehensive, fair, and accurate. I would enter only one caveat. That concerns his analysis of the economic mistake that was made by the incoming Irish government of 1977. The Irish economy was well into recovery by 1975, and Mr. McMahon claims that this new government "promised to spend the nation's way to new economic growth". The 1977 programme was not principally about increasing spending. In fact, it involved tax cuts, but the wrong kind of tax cuts. The taxation on motor cars was eliminated and so was the taxation on houses. These tax cuts had no beneficial economic effect. They were a windfall for car and house owners, and contributed to an import-led boom which caused big problems later on.

Achieving economic success is not simply a question of cutting taxes. It is a question of cutting the *right* taxes. The lesson of Irish economic history is that one should have a low and predictable rate of tax on the factors that generate growth. Companies and people at work generate growth. That is why the priority should be on reducing taxes on working people and on profits, rather than on reducing taxes on other activities. Ireland still has a pretty high rate of taxation on goods purchased in shops, but this has not inhibited economic growth.

The analysis of the impact of regional policy in this book is very important. In the European Union there is a commitment in the treaties to reducing regional disparities between poorer and richer parts of the Union. Mr. McMahon points out that in the United States "at no time has there been a commitment to reducing regional disparities."

Yet, in the United States, no matter how far a region falls, no matter how high unemployment soars, no matter how unique the problems, regional economies keep booming back. Because flexible labour markets tend to adjust quickly, regional recessions in the United States are usually short lived. In other parts of the world, a safety net intervenes to slow down the process of adjustment. This softens the blow but also prolongs the agony.

There should be a debate amongst policy-makers about the quality of government spending, as well as about quantity. Government spending programmes should promote flexibility. There should be an inbuilt mechanism to automatically adjust them to rises and falls in tax revenue. They should be designed so as not to carry forward existing commitments regardless of external economic circumstances. They should be focused on measurable improvements in services.

In Ireland we have tried through the Strategic Management Initiative (SMI) to improve the quality of government spending. Public-service agencies are supposed to set their own objectives and monitor their own performance against them. Unfortunately the objectives are often expressed in abstract and subjective terminology. In effect, the exam is so set that no one is allowed to fail.

My own experience in Ireland is that predictability is what business needs from government. One of the reasons for Ireland's economic success was that we have had a low corporate tax rate – previously 10 per cent now 12.5 per cent – which was guaranteed not to be changed by both government and opposition. If government, working with opposition, can guarantee predictable economic conditions, it will be doing the best it possibly can to help create economic success.

John Bruton TD
Former Prime Minister of Ireland (1994–97)
and Former Finance Minister (1981–82), (1986–87)

Introduction

Economic growth is not a mysterious force that strikes unpredictably or whose absence is inexplicable.

On the contrary, growth is the fruit of two forces: the ability of people to recognise opportunities, on the one hand, and the creation by government of a legal, fiscal, and regulatory framework in which it is worthwhile for people to exploit those opportunities. And since there is no shortage of energetic and entrepreneurial people wherever human beings are to be found, one of the most important factors explaining differences in economic performance will be public policy.

This book is about how a disparate platoon of economies – Ireland, the Netherlands, Georgia, Massachusetts, and Michigan – went from being laggards to economic stars. Their circumstances are all quite different. Ireland, for instance, was a perennial under-performer in a Europe full of sclerotic economies, and the Irish diaspora is eloquent testimony to the inability of generations of Irish to make a decent living at home. Massachusetts and Michigan, by contrast, were powerful economies laid low by vast changes in the structure of the U.S. economy. Holland became a victim of its own success when it allowed offshore natural-gas revenues to fund a huge expansion of the welfare state, destroying incentives to work in the process. And Georgia harnessed itself to social change (in the form of desegregation) and technological change (in the form of air-conditioning) to begin the long march out of economic stagnation that had characterised most of the American South for generations.

As different as their circumstances were, however, a certain number of common factors unite their happy experience with significant economic progress. They saw that trying to prop up dying industries was a mug's game. Public debt needed to be brought under control, taxes lowered, and excellent value offered in public services when measured against the taxes paid. Politics needed to be banished from decisions about where and how to invest, whether in public infrastructure or private industry. Work incentives needed to be improved by reforming social welfare. Profitability in the private sector needed to be improved. And costs, including labour costs, needed to be kept keenly competitive. The sum of these measures was a policy environment in which business had every reason to invest and build productive capacity, while workers had every reason to work hard and build their job skills. As the capital investment grew and workers became more skillful, real wages rose along with tax revenues, and a virtuous circle was created. Growth bred more growth, success bred more success.

In other words, what the examples Fred McMahon has gathered here show is what public-policy analysts have been saying for years: incentives and public policy matter. That should be comforting news for lagging regions, like Atlantic Canada, that are still searching for the key to success. That key is simply to put sensible policies in place, and then let the intelligence, industriousness, and ingenuity of people do the rest.

Brian Lee Crowley
President
Atlantic Institute for Market Studies

Executive Summary

This book is about what works economically – policies and approaches that have succeeded in bringing jobs and growth to economies which once faced crippling problems. The book examines Ireland, the Netherlands, Massachusetts, Michigan, and Georgia.

This is also something of a mystery story. Who, or what, beat the dickens out of once dynamic economies in the Netherlands, Massachusetts, and Michigan? What medicine did they take to become stronger economically than ever before? In cases like Ireland and the American Deep South, who or what was poisoning the well water, leaving these economies so weak for so long? What changed to transform such doddering wrecks into great wealth generators and job creators?

These economies vary hugely in structure, history, geography, and resource endowment. The causes of their economic problems also vary considerably, from deep policy mistakes in the Netherlands to the onset of fierce foreign competition that wrecked Michigan's economy.

This variation is a strength. It raises a most interesting question: Do successful economic polices, in such differing environments, have important elements of commonality that can be applied to other economies?

The strategy utilized in successful jurisdictions boils down to a surprisingly simple, even obvious, idea which can easily be duplicated, albeit in different forms, in widely varied economic jurisdictions.

Put simply, the strategy is to reduce costs in the economy, to allow investors to reap increased profits. In Ireland and the Netherlands, this was accomplished through tax reductions and cooperation between unions, business, and government in holding down wage growth. Even the union leadership argued in favour of wage moderation on the grounds that profits needed to be improved.

A similar story emerges in the United States. Georgia's powerful economic growth has been fuelled by low costs both in taxes and wages. State governments in Michigan and Massachusetts reduced expenditures and cut taxes to speed recovery.

Flexible, largely self-equilibrating labour markets in the United States put downward pressure on wages during recessions, reducing costs. This was the same result, wage moderation, as was achieved in Ireland and the Netherlands. In the United States, it occurred through market mechanisms. In Ireland and the Netherlands, it was accomplished through an explicit policy decision to rein in wages in favour of profits.

All this – lower taxes, wage moderation – opened more room for profits, which attracts further investment. Profits provide investors with the means for further investment and the incentive for increased investment. New investment generates jobs and wealth.

Still, this approach has been criticized as a "race to the bottom", sacrificing workers' income and government's ability to provide services. In fact, the exact opposite is true. Typically, tax cuts result in greater government revenues within a year or two, as increased growth quickly makes up for the cuts.

Similarly, *real* wages in Ireland and the Netherlands grew more rapidly after unions shifted from tough bargaining to a policy of wage moderation explicitly intended to increase business profits. This had two positive effects on longer-term wage growth. As investment, attracted by profits, increased, so too did the capital/labour ratio. This naturally made workers more productive and their labour more valuable. And, as employment grew, learning-by-doing and other forms of training also increased the value of labour. This created the room for real increases in wages that did not cut into profits, holding open the door to further investment and wage increases.

In the United States, relatively weak union power allows wages to adjust to changing economic conditions. In times of economic distress, wage growth in the United States weakens or declines much more readily than in Europe. This maintains profits. Yet, despite or because of weak unions, U.S. workers are the best paid in the world.

IRELAND

For generations, Ireland had been the most economically backward nation in northern Europe. Unable to generate enough prosperity and jobs for even its small population, Ireland exported people rather than goods and services. Independence did little to change this dismal situation. Ireland still lagged all its neighbours, and economic refugees continued to flee the island.

From independence to the late 1950s, Ireland tried to generate jobs by closing its economy and fostering import substitution. This was an unmitigated disaster. It only isolated Ireland from the powerful wave of growth and prosperity that swept through western Europe after the end of World War II. The results were so dismal that even the architects of the closed-door policy reversed course, opening the Irish economy to world competition at the end of the 1950s.

Thus began Ireland's first golden economic age. Ireland generated jobs and wealth faster than it ever had in its history. But this was a short-lived golden age. Skyrocketing public expenditure, soaring taxes, increased government intervention in the economy, bloated debts and deficits, and growing union militancy increased costs in the Irish economy. Profits virtually disappeared and so did investment. Unemployment rose and "the culture of employment" was lost to a whole sector of Irish society, people who joined the rolls of the long-term unemployed. As bad as things had been in the past, this proved to be the most dismal economic period in recent Irish economic history, for the earlier glimpse of prosperity had turned to ashes.

Bad times concentrated policy thinking. Irish society as a whole reached a consensus in the late 1980s that costs in the economy had to be reduced. Unions adopted wage moderation as their creed. Government slashed expenditures and taxes. Profits rose rapidly, creating a magnet for further investment.

The results were nothing short of miraculous. They did not simply better Ireland's own dismal economic history; Ireland's record of GDP growth is now the strongest in the developed world. In the early and mid-1980s, Irish unemployment had climbed to nearly 20 per cent. Now Ireland faces a labour shortage.

Tax cuts and wage moderation, far from reducing tax revenues and real wages, led to dramatic increases. Revenues are far higher now than when tax rates were at their peak. The Irish have gone from being one of the most poorly paid people in the developed world to one of the best paid. What many feared would be a "race to the bottom" became a rapid climb to new economic heights.

THE NETHERLANDS

The Dutch and the Irish economies followed similar roads to economic ruination. Then they took strikingly similar paths to economic salvation.

After the end of World War II, Dutch economic growth was powered by a society-wide agreement on wage moderation. This policy was so successful that, by the 1960s, Dutch labour markets were extremely tight, and workers found they could successfully demand much higher wages. The consensus on wage moderation collapsed, and wage costs soared.

At the same time, government hubris increased. Both taxes and expenditures skyrocketed. Unfortunately, expenditures had the faster take-off. The Netherlands began running huge deficits, which increased the cost of capital and costs related to uncertainty – fear of inflation and worry about high future taxes to pay off the debt. What followed was the worst period in Dutch peacetime economic history.

Slowly, through fits and starts in the 1980s and 1990s, the Dutch got their economic house back in order. Although a breakthrough labour agreement in 1982 ultimately failed in its goal of establishing durable wage moderation, further work in 1993 and 1994 succeeded in building a strong basis for moderation.

Similarly, the Dutch attack on government spending in the early

1980s faltered late in the decade. And it was never accompanied by a firm commitment to reduce taxes. The Wim Kok government, elected in 1994, changed all that, though Kok himself was the leader of the leftish Labour party. The new government forcefully tackled both expenditures and taxes. It has had considerable success in bringing both down.

It is the period after the aggressive reforms initiated in 1993 and 1994 to moderate wages and reduce taxes that became known as the time of the "Dutch miracle". As costs were reduced and profits restored in the Dutch economy, strong economic growth resumed. Real wages have increased. The Netherlands has gone from having one of the highest unemployment rates in Europe to one of the lowest anywhere in the world, and Dutch economic growth is again strong.

THE UNITED STATES

The United States has little in the way of regional programmes, yet regional problems do not endure long in the U.S. economy. Lagging regions have shown strong convergence with leading regions, and states tend to recover quickly from regional recessions.

The flexible labour market in the United States and low tax levels play important roles in this adjustment process. Moreover, the lack of regional programmes may be beneficial. Such programmes can artificially inflate a regional economy. This raises costs and replaces private-sector activity with public-sector activity. This shrinks the economic base and leaves the economy ever more dependent on government.

Two of the states examined, Michigan and Massachusetts, faced severe external shocks. For Michigan, it was foreign manufacturing competition. For Massachusetts, the winding down of the Cold War devastated the state's defence-contracting industry. As well, changes in technology destroyed the minicomputer industry, which was at the heart of Massachusetts's high-tech industry.

In both states, wages adjusted downwards in response to economic malaise. Both states also cut state government and reduced taxes. These factors made the states cost-competitive, drawing in new investment and powering the states' recovery. Both states have experienced powerful growth. Unemployment is lower now than it was before the onset of the regional recessions in Massachusetts and Michigan.

Georgia is a Deep South state, once the weakest economic regions in the United States. Georgia built its economic attractiveness on the twin pillars of low taxes and low wages. Now the state boasts one of the most dynamic economies in the world. Per capita state GDP exceeds the national average. Wages have grown strongly with new investment and are now higher than in Canada, yet low enough to permit healthy profits. This continues to power Georgia's growth.

Chapter 1
Policies That Work

This book is about what works economically – policies and approaches that have succeeded in bringing jobs and growth to economies which once faced crippling problems. Some less-successful economies will also be examined as a point of contrast for what works and what doesn't. In this sense, the book provides a practical guide to policy-makers of what to do and what not to do.

It could also be considered something of a mystery story. Who, or what, beat the dickens out of once dynamic economies in places like the Netherlands, Massachusetts, and Michigan? What medicine did they take to recover from their prosperity-threatening wounds to become stronger than ever before?

In cases like Ireland and the American Deep South, who or what was poisoning the well water, leaving these economies so weak for so long? What changed, virtually overnight, to transform such doddering wrecks into great wealth generators and job creators?

This book examines the star performers in the turn-around game. Just a few years ago, the Dutch and Irish economies were among the walking dead of Europe. Now, they've become two of the most successful economies in all of the developed world. Policy-makers and business journalists have fallen over themselves to coin handy monikers that capture this success. Thus was born the "Celtic Tiger" for Ireland, and the "Dutch Miracle" or "Polder Model" for the Netherlands.

The turn-arounds did not come accidentally or because of some fortuitous resource discovery, but rather because of consistent, deep, and widespread policy changes which reformed the Dutch and Irish economies from top to bottom. These policy changes will be fully examined in the chapters on Ireland and the Netherlands. Virtually the same set of reforms was launched in both nations, though the timing and depth of reform differed.

The extent of the turn-around in these two nations is hard to comprehend, especially that in Ireland. Ireland has long been one of Europe's most dismal performers, stuck on the periphery of the continent. Its chief export was its desperate, job-hungry people rather than any valued good or service. Just 15 years ago, things were even more desperate than usual in Ireland. Unemployment was soaring. Nearly one in five were without work. Ireland's deficit through the early 1980s averaged more than 12 per cent of GDP, about eight times the average rate of economic growth. The national debt soared.

Today, Ireland faces a labour shortage, and Irish recruiters scour the globe in an often-successful attempt to lure expatriates back home. The nation's debt melts away each year, and the vanishingly small deficit is less than a third the rate of economic growth. Government revenues have increased despite huge tax cuts. One comparison provides some idea of the speed of Ireland's growth in recent years. In the mid-1980s, Canada's per capita GDP was two and a half times the size of Ireland's. Now Irish per capita GDP exceeds Canada's.

Back in the 1970s, the Dutch were doing so poorly a new term entered the economic lexicon, "Dutch disease". This described the disastrous policy decisions that were strangling the Dutch economy. By 1984, unemployment had soared to over 17 per cent. The economy had been shedding thousands of jobs: between 1981 and 1983, nearly 300,000 jobs were lost. In 1984, 10,000 people were added a month to the unemployment rolls until the number reached 800,000.

Economic growth hovered close to zero through much of the 1980s. Dutch per capita GDP, which once exceeded the OECD average, continually lost ground and in 1980 fell below the OECD average. Dutch finances deteriorated badly. The deficit through much of the early 1980s was nearly 15 per cent of GDP.

The Dutch cure was remarkable. Unemployment has fallen to about 4 per cent, despite increasing participation in the work-force. The number of jobs in the Dutch economy swelled from five million in the mid-1980s to nearly seven million in the mid-1990s, and the number of jobs continues to increase.[1] The Dutch economy has been growing strongly, and per capita GDP again exceeds the OECD average. The Dutch budget is essentially balanced. The deficit is less than 1 per cent of GDP. As in Ireland, government revenues have increased despite tax cuts. The chapter on the Netherlands will examine the causes of Dutch disease and the policy changes that transformed Dutch disease into the Dutch Miracle.

In the United States, the Deep South held a position analogous to that of Ireland in Europe. The South was the perennial laggard, on the periphery of the U.S. economy, as isolated from the real economic action as Atlantic Canada is from that in the Canadian economy today. Georgia was a sleepy state in the deepest of the Deep South, along with its sister states of Alabama and Mississippi. Georgia's backwardness even turned up in popular songs: in "The Dock of the Bay", Otis Redding sang that he'd "left my home in Georgia [and] headed for the Frisco Bay" hoping for better times. Georgia was a "going down the road" state.

The amazing thing is that it requires some effort to recreate this mental picture of Georgia. Today, we think of Georgia as one of the most advanced economies anywhere. Atlanta boasts a spectacular skyline. Many of the world's most dynamic companies are headquartered there. Tens of millions of people see pictures from Atlanta every day on the Atlanta-based CNN. Georgia's economy creates between 100,000 and 150,000 additional jobs each year. Between 1980 and 1996, Georgia's per capita GDP soared from

---

1. These numbers are from the U.S. Bureau of Labor Statistics, which uses a standardized definition. I use these data to get a consistent measure across differing economies. The Dutch statistics show fewer jobs both back in the 1970s and today.

86 per cent of the U.S. national average to 106 per cent of the national average. U.S. economic growth may have been strong, but Georgia's was that much stronger.

In the 1980s and early 1990s, Massachusetts suffered crippling blows to its essential high-tech sector. Through the 1980s, the mini-computer industry had been the centrepiece of the Massachusetts high-tech sector. That industry essentially collapsed in the late 1980s and the early 1990s, pushed out of the office by personal computers and workstations. The end of the Cold War decimated Massachusetts's huge defence industry. The malaise spread well beyond the high-tech sector. Businesses were collapsing or fleeing the state for any number of reasons, including sky-rocketing taxes that had earned the state the nickname "Tax-achusetts".

By the late 1980s, employment had stopped growing in Massachusetts. In just 12 months – from mid-1990 to mid-1991 – Massachusetts lost over 200,000 jobs. Unemployment soared to nearly 10 per cent, and would have gone much higher if hundreds of thousands of workers had not left the work-force and the state. Here again, the turn-around has been dramatic. Since 1991, the Massachusetts economy has added nearly half a million jobs. Unemployment has fallen below 4 per cent. Workers have an easier time finding a job than employers have finding workers.

Michigan's fall from economic grace was so great that it got a name. Michigan was the epicentre of the U.S. "rust belt". Michigan's economy was built on the automotive industry, and in the 1970s the U.S. automotive industry was headed for a devastating wreck. By the early 1980s, the rustbelt was no mere concept; it was a vivid image of the Michigan landscape, dotted by closed and rusting factories, which had once spun out the state's prosperity. In less than three years, from mid-1979 to the beginning of 1983, Michigan lost nearly half a million jobs. Unemployment soared to 16 per cent. The turn-around has been remarkable. Since 1983, over 1.4 million jobs have been created in Michigan. The state's unemployment rate has fallen to under 5 per cent. That's even lower than Michigan unemployment before the onset of the rustbelt era.

As a point of contrast, the book examines several less-success-ful economies, to see what marks successful policy off from un-successful policy. Louisiana has lagged far behind other south-ern states, making it a natural choice for comparison. Why has this southern state, the one with the most obvious economic potential – situated at the nexus of one of the world's great trans-portation routes, the Mississippi River, blessed by immense natu-ral-resource wealth, and benefiting from a large population and domestic market – failed to match the growth and job creation found in its less-well-endowed neighbours?

Maine provides a convenient point of comparison with Massa-chusetts. Maine tends to go up and down with the Massachusetts's economy, yet it has not fully shared Massachusetts's revival, nor has its convergence towards the national level of economic activ-ity matched the record of other lagging states.

This selection of jurisdictions provides several advantages. It includes economies that have overcome long-term, historic weak-nesses (Ireland and the Deep South), as well as jurisdictions which recovered from crippling economic downturns (the Netherlands, Michigan, and Massachusetts).

It provides a taste of the different flavours of today's market economy. Among the Western world's major economies, the United States has the least fettered markets and the smallest gov-ernment. The Irish and Dutch economies are fundamentally mar-ket economies, but they are influenced by powerful corporatist entities representing labour, business and government. These groups can collectively manipulate market signals, particularly labour-market signals. They can negotiate broad agreements on nation-wide wage levels. For this reason, these economies are of-ten classified as "corporatist" (see Appendix).

The mix of jurisdictions examined also provides an interesting range of political settings, from the right-wing environment of the Deep South, to hard-to-classify Irish politics, to the soft-left-wing Dutch milieu, where the 1990s reformist government was headed by a former union leader, who had led the largest federation of Dutch unions.

This selection also makes it possible to distinguish between what might loosely be termed "man-made" economic disasters versus "natural" economic disasters. Both the Dutch and Irish economic problems fall into the first category. Economic problems were largely self-inflicted. The Dutch economy had been one of the most successful in post-war Europe, while the Irish economy, for the first time in its history, experienced strong sustained growth in the 1960s. In both cases, a disastrous policy mix knocked the economy off its growth course.

Michigan comes closest to having suffered a "natural" economic disaster, in that state policy-makers obviously had nothing to do with the onslaught of foreign competition that decimated the automotive industry. Massachusetts suffered from a mix of bad policy and bad times in its technology sector. Georgia sat on a pile of historical weaknesses, not the least of which was racism, which not only deprived the state of the full use of the talents of all its citizens, but also set group against group in an effort, on one side, to protect privilege and, on the other, to achieve fair treatment.

The number of different jurisdictions examined does create one difficulty. Identical data series are not available for each jurisdiction, and this limits data comparisons in some cases. As well, some of the problems and structures will not have exact parallels in all economies. This means each jurisdiction may be painted in slightly different hues.

Despite this weakness, the variation in type of economic problem, economic structure, and political background is important. It raises a most interesting question: Do successful economic polices, in such differing environments, have important elements of commonality that can be applied to other economies?

COSTS

Indeed they do. While the type of economic structure and problems examined vary a great deal, the strategy utilized in successful jurisdictions boils down to a surprisingly simple, even obvious idea which can easily be duplicated, albeit in different forms, in widely varied economic jurisdictions. Put simply, the strategy is to reduce costs in the economy to allow investors to reap increased profits, thus encouraging further investment, increased productivity, and, ultimately, higher wages.[2] In the Netherlands and Ireland, this was accomplished through tax reductions, and cooperation between unions, business, and government in holding down wage growth. Even the union leadership argued in favour of wage moderation on the grounds that profits needed to be improved.

A similar story emerges in the United States. Georgia's powerful economic growth has been fuelled by low costs, both in taxes and wages. State governments in Michigan and Massachusetts reduced expenditures and taxes to boost economic growth. Flexible, largely self-equilibrating labour markets in the United States put downward pressure on wages during recessions, reducing costs. This was the same result as was achieved in Ireland and the Netherlands. In the United States, it occurred through market mechanisms. In Ireland and the Netherlands, it was accomplished through an explicit policy decision, supported by unions, to rein in wages in favour of profits.

All this – lower taxes, wage moderation – opened more room for profits, which attracts further investment. Higher profits provide investors with the means for further investment and the incentive for increased investment. New investment generates jobs and wealth. Still, this approach has been criticized as one that amounts to a race to the bottom, sacrificing workers' income and government's ability to provide services. In fact, the exact opposite is true. Typically tax cuts within a year or two result in greater government revenues, as increased growth quickly makes up for

---

2. Other views of development can also be viewed under the rubric of *costs*. For example, the idea of economic clusters, most famously the software cluster in Silicon Valley, is partly based on the idea of cost advantage. Finding and recruiting essential personnel is easier and cheaper within a geographic cluster of similar industries. Not finding the right skills can be hugely costly. The same holds true of access to suppliers and customers. Clusters are also powered by a diffusion of ideas and expertise, but this is another way of saying that essential information can be more inexpensively obtained within a cluster.

the cuts. This is exactly what happened in each of the jurisdictions examined in this book.

Similarly, as we shall see, *real* wages in the Netherlands and Ireland grew more strongly after unions shifted from tough bargaining to a policy of wage moderation explicitly intended to increase business profits. This had two positive effects on longer-term wage growth. As investment, attracted by profits, increased, so too did the capital/labour ratio. This naturally made workers more productive and their labour more valuable. And, as employment grew, learning-by-doing and other forms of training also increased the value of labour. This created the room for real increases in wages that did not cut into profits, holding open the door to further investment and wage increases.

It is important to contrast this approach with the negotiating militancy that both Irish and Dutch unions abandoned in the 1980s. In any given year, unions would negotiate for as much as they could get. Businesses, rather than close down, would agree to high wages, even if it meant profits were virtually eliminated, as they were in Ireland and the Netherlands. That deprived businesses of the means and the incentive for further investment. Productivity stagnated. In the next round of tough bargaining, businesses would have little extra to give workers in real terms. Nominal wages were forced up, but gains were eaten away by inflation, since the economy itself had no more wealth to spread around. Through this period, Irish and Dutch real wages stagnated or fell.

Now Dutch and Irish unions calibrate wage demands to leave employers strong profits, generating future investment. In other words, they are careful not to kill the golden goose which provides the means for wage increases in future years. Now Irish and Dutch wages are on a steady upward path, maintained paradoxically by a bargaining strategy in which unions refrain from seeking the maximum possible settlement in any given year.

CONVERGENCE

Half a century of empirical research confirms powerful theoretical reasons to believe that lagging economies naturally catch up with advanced ones. This is an optimistic prediction. It says that, even if advanced nations are growing quickly, lagging regions should grow more quickly.

Convergence is due to the spread of productive ideas and methods, profit opportunities in under-invested economies, lower wages that draw capital, and increasing skills as investment creates jobs. A key mechanism here is the idea of labour/capital ratio. When labour is abundant relative to capital, labour costs should be relatively low and potential returns, profits, on the scarce resource, capital, should be relatively high. The profit motive attracts capital and creates jobs and economic growth. This mechanism can be derailed by policies that either inflate the cost of labour or reduce returns on capital.

The same story applies to human capital – education and training – though here human capital may increase not merely by added investment in human capital but also by an indirect route – learning-by-doing. As workers become accustomed to working in non-traditional industries, their productivity improves. The process continues as capital is added. This could be regarded as investment by workers and the firm in human capital, or simply as a positive externality of investment-driven economic growth.

Not all economies join the convergence club, though. In fact, the gap between most rich and poor nations has been growing. Membership in the convergence club is straightforward. Economies which have been closing the gap with advanced economies have a number of shared characteristics – an educated populace (or at least an emphasis on education in public policy that is reflected by a large commitment to improving the educational standing of the populace),[3] market economy, limited government

---

3. Canada spends a larger portion of its national output on education than any other country in the OECD yet has, by some accounts, the lowest rate of productivity growth of all these countries. One of the problems with measuring the quality of education is that the level of expenditure correlates poorly (if at all) with the actual output of the system. Thus, measuring expenditure provides a poor indicator of quality. How education is delivered seems much more important than how much is spent.

interference in markets, the rule of law, property rights, and stable institutions, including political stability. For the most part, economies that lack these characteristics are either failing to converge with richer nations or, more typically, are falling further behind them. However, while it is true to say that in much of the world the gap between rich and poor is increasing, what this really reflects is a growing gap between market and non-market economies. The story is exactly the opposite among market economies, where the gap is narrowing.

In regions characterized by market economies, the "convergence effect" shows up strongly in econometric testing, whether in U.S. states, European regions, or Japanese prefectures. All a lagging region needs is a sensible policy regime – one no worse, or not much worse, than those advanced regions. There is the rub. Lagging regions can be held behind by bad policy. For example, Atlantic Canada, which will be studied in the second volume of this book, has converged with the rest of Canada at only one-third to half the rate of convergence in the United States, Europe, and Japan, although Atlantic Canada has received from the federal government huge wealth transfers and development programmes meant to spur economic growth.

There's even better news from within developing nations. Econometric testing shows that economic growth, instead of increasing inequalities, raises incomes across the board, reducing absolute poverty and improving social conditions, as measured by the proxy of infant mortality.

> Development economists used to worry that the benefits of growth would be undone by increases in income inequality. Recent evidence has shown conclusively, however, that this is not so.... [One] study examined recent per capita growth and poverty reduction in 67 countries for which household data were available. It found that every country with increasing per capita household income saw poverty decline, and every country with declining per capita income saw poverty increase. In the

expanding economies, per capita income grew 4 percent, and poverty declined 5 percent. In declining economies an average drop of 7 percent in per capita income lead to an increase in poverty of 19 percent .... (Dollar & Pritchett 1998, 39)[4]

A review of the literature finds strong empirical support for the convergence hypothesis. (See, for example, Baumol et al. 1994, for a wide-ranging selection of articles on the subject, including literature reviews.) Perhaps the most comprehensive examination of the convergence hypothesis, both for modelling and for empirical investigation, is found in Barro and Sala-i-Martin (1995).

Barro and Sala-i-Martin develop data and examine economic performance in three different theatres: among U.S. states since 1880, Japanese prefectures since 1930, and regions within eight European nations since 1950. They find a convergence rate of between 2 and 3 per cent a year in each of these areas. The convergence effect is absolute; i.e., it applies when no explanatory variable other than the initial level of per capita GDP or income is held constant. This means that, each year, a lagging region closes the gap with the leading economy by between 2 and 3 per cent. Convergence is, therefore, a relatively slow process: it would take 25 to 35 years to close the gap by one half. The various authors whose work appears in Baumol (1994) find similar results for the regions they examine. However, several of these authors find a slow-down in the convergence effect after 1973, when productivity growth suffered a world-wide slow-down. But, Barro and Sala-i-Martin note, their results do not reject the possibility that the

---

4. In the section quoted, Dollar and Pritchett refer to Burnside and Dollar (1998) (see references). They also site two other studies, not used as references in this work, which reach similar conclusions on the impact of economic growth: Li, Hongyi, Lyn Squire, and Heng-fu Zou. 1998. "Explaining International and Intertemporal Variations in Income Inequality". *Economic Journal* 108; and Bruno, Michael, Martin Ravallion, and Lyn Squire. 1998. "Equity and Growth in Developing Countries: Old and New Perspectives on the Policy Issues", in V. Tanzi and K. Chu (eds.) *Income Distribution and High-quality Growth*. Cambridge, MA:MIT Press.

convergence effect is invariant over time, at least as far as the United States is concerned.

Barro and Sala-i-Martin, like other researchers in the field, find that convergence is not unconditional, but rather is influenced by a number of factors, specifically policy factors:

> Growth depends positively on the initial quantity of human capital in the form of educational attainment and health, negatively on the ratio of government consumption spending to GDP, and negatively on measures of distortions of markets and political instability.... In most cases, the empirical work does not provide robust estimates for the effects of specific government policies on growth, but it does show that the overall package of policies matters a lot. (Barro & Sala-i-Martin 1995, 6-7)

TAXES AND PUBLIC SERVICES

All successful jurisdictions examined in this book used tax cuts to spur growth. Moreover, the global evidence on convergence shows high government expenditures and high taxes impede growth. This section will examine a broad range of research on the impact of taxes and government expenditures.

At first glance, the evidence on taxes and public services might seem contradictory. The evidence unambiguously shows that low taxes and low government consumption promote growth. It also shows that so do strong public services. But, to get strong public services, taxes and spending have to be sufficiently high. Obviously, the key here is efficiency and productivity – to get the highest possible level of public service for the lowest possible cost. In other words, since high taxes suppress growth but good public services and investment spur growth, government must spend carefully to get a dollar's value for a dollar spent.

Tom Cunningham, vice-president of the Federal Reserve Bank of Atlanta, argues that the key to providing good government – combined with strong growth and employment creation – is to keep government on the efficiency frontier, the idea again being that government provide the highest level of services possible for the lowest cost.[5] "In Georgia, we have a weak education system, but we keep taxes very low. So we're getting what we pay for. In Minnesota and Wisconsin, they have high taxes but they provide strong services which compensates for the high tax load."

A couple of caveats need to be provided, on both sides of the spending equation. At some point, even with careful spending, government runs out of worthwhile things to do, and spending itself becomes a drag on the economy. By bidding up the price of scarce resources, it crowds out other activity, including investment, without producing any significant benefits. On the other hand, up to some point, increased government spending, if efficient, boosts the economy. Growth would be stifled in any jurisdiction where the government did not tax enough to fund roads, schools, public protection, etc.

Barro and Sala-i-Martin, based on their empirical research, model this type of relationship. While the model is too complex to develop mathematically in this type of book, the concepts can be intuitively understood through an examination of Figure 1 (Barro and Sala-i-Martin 1995, 152-61). This represents the relationship between the size of government and the economy's growth rate: G represents government, Y represents per capita economic activity, τ represents the size of government (G/Y), and γ represents the rate of per capita economic growth. At low rates of government spending the marginal product of more spending is high, as is its effect on capital's marginal product (for example, through further education improving the productivity of the work force). This outweighs the distorting effect of taxes. Thus, the economy's growth rates rises with τ, though as τ moves up the curve, the distorting effect of taxes becomes stronger relative to the effect of more τ on capital, until it reaches a peak and begins to decline.[6]

The same diagram can be used to capture Cunningham's

---

5. From a conversation with the author.

6. Also see King and Rebelo (1990) for a model which shows large effects from taxation in an endogenous growth model, much larger than in a neoclassical model.

Figure 1

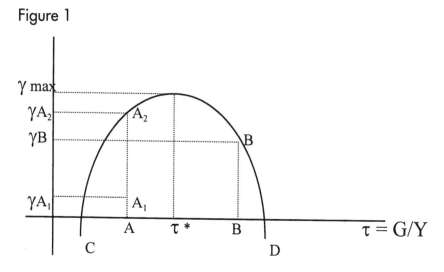

insight, though the Barro–Sala-i-Martin mathematical model would have to be modified to do it. The CD curve might be imagined as representing an efficiency frontier. Each point inside the curve represents a less-than-efficient use of government resources. Any point inside the curve, such as A_1, represents a suboptimum mix of government spending. At A_1, the economy obtains only an $A_1 \gamma$ rate of growth though for the same level of government spending, an γA_2 rate of growth could be achieved. A number of extensions would be required to capture these effects, but this provides an intuitive sense of the discussion.

Just considering transportation infrastructure for the moment, one might imagine that, at A_1, a certain portion of road spending is distributed as a political reward. The positive economic impact of this is small. Thus, economic growth is slowed by the distorting effect of taxes while not benefiting from the full potential of investment.[7] On the other hand, A_2 might be imagined as a point where all road spending is used to improve the transportation infrastructure, for example, building a more efficient highway to

---

7. Of course, in a case like this, both taxes and the resulting spending are likely to introduce distortions, weakening growth from both the expenditure and taxation sides of the government balance sheet.

the region's markets. This improves the returns on investment in the region by providing a more efficient transportation infrastructure and regional growth benefits.

This discussion leads to the problem of measuring the impact of taxes and services. The amount of tax revenue collected is relatively easy to measure, but some tax systems are better than others. It becomes very difficult to construct variables that both capture the intake of the tax system and provide a measure of the system's efficiency, but at least a number of conceptual tools are available when one examines a tax system. Similarly, it is easy to judge total expenditures and determine which types of expenditure are good (infrastructure, for example) and which are bad (spending on political rewards, for example).

But no budget breaks transportation spending into categories such as "Road construction: Infrastructure improvement" and "Road construction: Cabinet minister's constituency". For example, an examination of infrastructure spending in Atlantic Canada would not reveal that the region never funded a modern highway to Atlantic Canada's major inland market in central Canada, despite government expenditures typically equallng about two-thirds of GDP (see McMahon 2000). Nor has public policy in Atlantic Canada focused on building a major highway to the region's emerging market in New England, thus connecting into the efficient U.S. highway infrastructure. The problem of determining the quality of government spending becomes intractable if only government books are available. Is a new hospital being built to improve health care or improve the governing party's chances of being elected in a swing constituency?[8]

Despite these complications, a number of researchers have attempted to quantify the impact of taxes and government services on economic growth and job creation. Wasylenko (1997) examines 38 econometric studies of the impact of taxation on per capita

---

8. The probability of the latter being the case approaches 1 if an adequate new hospital is built and the old hospital down the road is also kept open in a small community, as has happened in Nova Scotia.

GDP in U.S. states. Of these, 23 report statistically significant elasticities, with median values ranging from –0.58 to –0.02,[9] though he notes "several carefully done studies by respected researchers find tax elasticities larger than ... –0.6" (45). This is balanced by the fact that "at least an equal number of researchers" find small or statistically insignificant elasticities. Overall, he argues, the studies taken together suggest an elasticity of about –0.20 for interregional studies.[10] Yet Wasylenko also notes that World Bank research consistently shows that low-tax developing countries outperform high-tax developing countries. Wasylenko suspects one reason for the weak results in studies of the United States is the similarity of tax regimes across the country:

> [S]tates and regions have acted to neutralize the effect of taxes by adopting tax systems that are more alike. Without significant differences in state tax systems, taxes will not play a significant role in firm location and expansion. Given any particular tax elasticity estimate, however, the degree to which a specific state's tax rate will affect economic activity in the state depends on the degree to which a state's tax burden deviates from that in relevant comparison states. As long as the tax elasticity is negative and significantly different from zero, high tax states will lose more economic activity than average or low-tax states. Indeed, the highest tax states, such as Minnesota, Wisconsin and New York have recently acknowledged that high taxes may be responsible for low rates of job creation in those states. (Wasylenko 1997, 47-48)

---

9. The negative sign indicates a negative relationship between tax levels and GDP growth. For example, with an elasticity of –0.60 means a 0.10 (10 per cent) increase in taxes reduces per capita GDP by 6 per cent (0.10 x –0.60 = –0.06).

10. Wasylenko's review of intraregional studies suggests an intra-regional elasticity of about –0.80, while Bartik (1997, 67) puts it slightly higher at –1.0 to –3.0. Bartik's range for interregional elasticity, –0.10 to –0.60, is consistent with Wasylenko.

The homogeneity of tax regimes in the United States may make it difficult to pick up tax effects – though they are still evident in the majority of the research, and policy-makers in states such as Michigan and Massachusetts believe tax reductions helped power their recoveries – but international comparisons are more revealing, Wasylenko notes. These results are consistent with the studies on convergence and foreign aid, which point to government consumption as a strong negative factor affecting growth.

Fisher (1997) reviews the other side of the balance sheet: the impact of government services on economic growth. He looks at three service variables: highway and transportation facilities, public safety, and education. He notes that, of 15 econometric studies on transportation infrastructure, ten find a positive effect from such spending, with eight of these reporting a statistically significant impact. Of nine studies reviewed on public-safety spending, four report statistically significant positive results. Of 19 studies reviewed on education spending, 12 show a positive relationship but only six report a statistically significant positive relationship. One problem with this measure is that other tests have found little or no relationship between the quality of education and the amount spent on it, so the spending variable used in these tests is a poor proxy for what needs to be measured: educational outcomes rather than money inputs.

This may appear surprising, since the quality of labour is almost always on the top of the list in factors firms cite as important in making investment decisions. This highlights the disconnection researchers have found between the level of education spending and education outcomes. The fact that the level of spending appears to have little or no effect on educational attainment has been known since the late 1960s and is supported by the most recent comprehensive studies.[11] It appears that the approach to education matters much more than the actual amount spent, but

---

11. See, for example, the series of studies produced in recent years by the International Association for the Evaluation of Educational Achievement, *Third International Mathematics and Science Studies*. This effort involves between about 20 and 40 nations and usually significantly above 1,000 schools and 10,000 students and includes both international and intranational comparisons.

the econometric studies measure only spending. Fisher points to additional reasons for the surprising results: the lag between changes in the educational system and the effect on adult participants in the labour force, wide variations within states on educational spending, and the many different variables that effect educational achievement.

Both Fisher, on the expenditure side, and Wasylenko, on the taxation side, also note the problem discussed above – the weakness of any study that examines taxes and services in isolation from each other. This reflects the idea of cost. It's not simply the price tag – tax level – which is important, but the worth of the goods and services obtained for that price which determines whether the tax load provides good value.

Ady, who, as an executive consultant with Deloitte & Touche/ Fantus, has practical experience in such matters, points this out when he discusses the final selection process for a site:

> At this level of the analysis, the "services" side of taxes is also carefully measured – what the company will receive for its tax dollars in the way of services, such as police protection, education capabilities, and the like. For our clients, education has been found to be the single most important service, greatly exceeding the value of all other services combined. A distant second is highway adequacy, followed by public safety and then infrastructure. (Ady 1997, 79)

He then discusses how firms judge the quality of the services. One striking fact is that the measures are largely unrelated to spending amounts, but instead focus on factors which provide an indication of outcome, such as SAT/ACT scores. For example, in the relationship between education and the quality of the available work-force, he says,

> [B]ased on our practical experience, the single most important determinant of the potential of labor quality in an

area is the presence of post-high school educational facilities, along with the degree to which these institutions are working with local businesses to meet their recruitment needs. (Ady 1997, 81)

Nonetheless, Ady says firms pay careful attention to the overall tax burden, and high tax rates may eliminate a jurisdiction even before the actual burden for the firm is calculated: "Taxes will be brought into the analysis but only on a comparative basis.... If any state is not reasonably competitive with the others based on these general tax inputs, it will probably be eliminated at this [preliminary] stage. For example, if most states in the defined area of search have corporate tax levies of 5 or 6 per cent but one has a 10 per cent levy, the latter state may be eliminated, even though the actual corporate taxes for the project have not been calculated" (Ady 1997, 78). But these comments should be put beside Ady's view that, among U.S. states, taxes are a small part of overall costs. For that reason, they are rarely the key determining factor in location decisions, and the importance of taxes – unless the taxes in one jurisdiction are significantly out of line with neighbouring jurisdictions – can only be judged in relation to the service being provided.

In conclusion, most studies show that taxes have an impact on economic growth, but that this impact is small unless the tax regimes are significantly different. This is a problem in Atlantic Canada, where taxes are much higher than elsewhere in Canada and where the quality of services provided in return is suspect, as we shall see in *Retreat from Growth: Atlantic Canada's Dismal Experience with Regional Development*, the sequel to this book.

In Massachusetts policy-makers believe that, through the 1980s, taxes in Massachusetts had risen to such a level – the state became known as Tax-achusetts – they did discourage economic growth and job creation. Yet the impact of taxes can only be examined in relation to the services provided. This does emphasize the need for good governance which focuses on providing essential services at the lowest possible cost.

LABOUR

The quality of labour, the cost of labour, and the state of the labour market, together, are essential to economic growth. The key question is whether the cost of labour in one jurisidiction is competitive with that in other jurisdictions. Any number of competitiveness studies compare wages and salaries across different jurisdictions. But these studies have a central failing. Two engineers of apparently similar qualifications may have very different levels of skills. Variable factors include work culture, degree-granting institution, years worked, sub-field, etc. Consider two computer engineers with, for simplicity's sake, degrees from the same institution. One works in Silicon Valley and has specialized in advanced applications; the other returned to Wyoming, took several years off to try ranching, and now runs the aging mainframe system of a regional business. A competitiveness study would indicate the Wyoming engineer, who is doubtless paid less than the Silicon Valley engineer, has the more competitive pay rate. Such a competitiveness study would likely show that Wyoming is a more competitive location for a software maker than Silicon Valley.

Cross-national or even cross-regional comparisons just can't pick up even broadly spread differences in work culture, regional educational quality, workplace opportunities which advance human capital, etc. Yet wage levels are obviously important, as we shall see, though companies try to evaluate regional work-forces by the compensation rates taken in conjunction with skills and work habits, something competitiveness studies typically do not handle comprehensively. Thus, these studies are not terribly useful in examining the impact of wages on economic growth.

The safest relative comparisons are wages of the same labour force compared over short time horizons. If real wage rates escalate over the short term, for example, because of union pressure, government stimulus, or external wealth transfers, then it is fairly safe to say wage rates are less competitive than they were. Even if real wage gains prove to be transitory, due to accompanying inflation, the lack of wage stability and the worry of future wage shocks becomes a disincentive to invest. On the other hand, if real wages decline in relation to productivity (say, because unions agree to wage restraint), then one can with relative safety say wages have become more competitive, particularly if this development holds the promise of future wage stability.

In a market-oriented economy, wages will change in response to market conditions. But these changes can be overridden by other factors. This is particularly true in a corporatist economy, where unions, business, and government may strike deals that have a large influence on wage settlements. The other possibility is a flexible labour market, where wages adjust rapidly in response to changing economic conditions. For any number of reasons, no labour market is perfectly flexible, but many economists believe that the rates of unemployment in the United Kingdom and the United States are much lower than those in continental Europe in large measure because the former have much more flexible labour markets.

For example, it is typically easier to fire or lay off someone in the United States than in Europe. European-style policies thus maintain existing jobs, but they dampen job creation. Firms have difficulty adjusting to changing conditions. During a downturn, they may not be able to make appropriate staffing adjustments, cutting into profits or creating losses. As well, firms become reluctant to hire in good times because, if a downturn occurs, a firm may not be able to adjust its labour force. Thus, such inflexibility in the labour market weakens firms' growth prospects and profits. It leaves firms with less money to invest and less incentive to invest. And this has a negative impact on job creation.

Another aspect of labour-force flexibility concerns the degree of union penetration and power, and the attitude of the union leadership. In Ireland and the Netherlands, unions have significant power over wage settlements, but the attitude of the union leadership in recent years directed this power towards the goal of wage moderation. In the United States, relatively low levels of union membership weaken union influence over wages and allows the labour market to adjust to changing economic conditions, including by moderating wage demands during economic downturns. These are essential points in later chapters, so it is important to examine the impact of unions on wages and labour market flexibility.

Many economists argue that union power distorts the labour market and weakens productivity gains, thus slowing growth and job creation. Mancur Olsen has a slightly different take on union power. He argues that either high or low levels of union power produce benefits but that moderate levels of union membership and power are likely to damage an economy.

While Olsen accepts the idea that unions may harm economic growth, he argues that, when an economy is largely unionized, the labour movement may accept responsibility for the general welfare of the economy. This benefits all workers, not just unionized workers. This is what Ireland and the Netherlands have experienced in recent years as their central union bodies officially adopted the wage-moderation policy. In both nations, union and non-union employment has grown rapidly.

But Olsen believes that when unions have substantial clout, but not an overarching interest in the economy, they may introduce substantial distortions in the economy through rent-seeking activities for their members – benefits beyond the level that their productivity would justify – which reduces general welfare. In this case, union power may force wages to a level incompatible with full employment, whereas in the former case, unions may adopt a policy of wage moderation which generates employment across the economy.

Olsen's insight has been repeated in many different forms, which have somewhat different implications but maintain the central insight. One idea is that "[e]xtreme centralisation or decentralisation of bargaining encourages wage moderation in collective bargaining, whereas intermediate union structures are associated with wage demands inconsistent with high employment."[12] As well, the insider–outsider hypothesis has been used as an "explanation of upwardly ratcheting unemployment rates in Europe.... [U]nions and other institutions tend to represent the interests of 'insiders'(job-holders) at the expense of outsiders (the unemployed)" (Burda 1997, 96).

Clearly, powerful unions may contribute to economic growth by promoting wage moderation, which generates jobs, profits, investment, and economic growth. We'll see this in Ireland and the Netherlands. But what about the other side of Olsen's idea – that a medium level of union power suppresses growth more than weak union power? One way to explore this idea is to examine the impact of right-to-work laws in the 21 U.S. states that have such laws. These laws prohibit unions from imposing membership on workers in unionized workplaces. In the 29 non–right-to-work states, workers are required to join a union and pay dues as a condition of employment in unionized shops. This provides a point of comparison between jurisdictions with moderate union power (at least in the U.S. context) and those with weak union power, the right-to-work states.

Tannewald (1997) notes that a number of econometric studies – eight of the 11 reviewed – have found "that the existence of a right-to-work law exerts a positive, statistically significant impact on economic activity." On the other hand, Tannewald argues, studies have not produced convincing evidence that right-to-work laws either diminish unionization or lead to lower wages. One possible explanation is that unions are less militant in right-to-work states, creating flexibility in the workplace, which could increase economic growth, and that employers pay union-level wages regardless, to ensure labour peace and a sense of fairness.

Holmes (1996) attempted to overcome econometric problems by presenting a very simple test. Cutting across the United States runs something very much like a continuous border which sepa-

---

12. Burda (1997, 96) refers this concept to Calmfors, L., and J. Driffill. 1988. "Bargaining Structure, Corporatism and Macroeconomic Performance." *Economic Policy* 6: 13-62.

rates southern and western right-to-work states from northeastern and midwest non–right-to-work states. Another western border separates the Pacific states, which don't have right-to-work laws, from the western states, which do. Holmes finds large differences between the two sides of the border: "The differences at the border are surprisingly big. On average, the manufacturing share of total employment in a county increases by about a third when one crosses the border to the [right-to-work] side" (Holmes 1996, 28-29).

Even some union economists accept this view. For example, Jim Stanford, of the Canadian Auto Workers, writes: "Anti-union 'right-to-work' laws in the Deep South states of the U.S. have clearly been important in motivating a significant migration of manufacturing investment to those states from the free-association states of the northern part of that country" (Stanford 1999, 172).

Yet there are many anecdotal instances of unions and management working together to improve productivity and competitiveness, on one side, and working conditions on the other. This depends on a dynamic developing where employers and workers come to believe they both prosper or suffer together – where unions believe only a productive, competitive, profitable business can maintain their jobs and increase pay, while company officials understand the company's future depends on the quality and co-operation of labour.

In both Ireland and the Netherlands, large union groups played a key role in reforms that were explicitly designed to stabilize labour costs and increase profits. In both nations, the unions had come to believe that weak profits were stifling investment and job creation and that they needed to expand their focus to the whole state of the economy.

CASE STUDIES

The economies selected for examination in this book were chosen because of their strong growth following either a significant setback or a long period as a lagging region. The goal is to isolate successful turn-around strategies. In all these successful cases of economic growth, policy-makers focused on reducing the costs facing business and, particularly in the corporatist setting, on strategies explicitly meant to boost business profits. This is also true of turn-around economies not examined in this book, whether in Europe (for example, Denmark) or in the United States (for example, California).

In corporatist states, government policy-makers can not only tackle the cost of taxes, they can also deal with wage levels through the social partners – business and the labour movement. This is important, since market signals can easily be overridden in the corporatist state, halting wage adjustment when economic conditions changed. This happened in during the bad times in the Netherlands and Ireland.

U.S. states typically have flexible labour markets. This itself is an inducement to growth or a path to recovery, since wage levels adjust to economic circumstances. However, policy-makers in the United States can attempt to further the flexibility of the labour market. In both Michigan and Massachusetts, as part of these states' response to their economic downturn, the government reduced labour-market regulation and cut payroll taxes.[13]

All successful jurisdictions, in both Europe and the United States, focused on the cost of government. Through their economic advance to increased prosperity, southern states have long positioned themselves as low-tax jurisdictions. In both Michigan and Massachusetts, policy-makers came to believe that levels of taxation that were relatively high, at least in the U.S. setting, were holding back economic growth and job creation. This view was widely shared among the people of these states, who elected governors and legislators committed to tax reduction.

The corporatist states took even broader measures to reduce labour and tax costs. In both nations examined, comprehensive deals were struck to hold down wage growth. Both nations also moved to reduce taxes, the Netherlands more recently and less

---

13. The role of regulation is only touched on lightly in this book. It is the central focus on an upcoming AIMS book by Brian Flemming, a former senior aide to Prime Minister Pierre Trudeau.

aggressively than Ireland. Both nations are now addressing the problem of the long-term unemployed or, in the Netherlands, the long-term disabled. The Dutch disability system was, in effect, open to anyone who claimed to be disabled, and it offered generous payments. At one point, one million of six million Dutch workers were collecting disability. Both Ireland and the Netherlands are addressing the long-term unemployed/disabled problem by tightening restrictions on social payments, reducing the payments, and increasing the take-home pay of low-paid workers, either directly through subsidies or through reforms in the tax system designed to reduce the effective tax rates imposed on low-income earners.

The hope is to create a more flexible labour market by reducing incentives to stay out of the labour market, eliminating disincentives to join the labour market (such as the loss of secondary benefits) and increasing the take-home pay of workers, without increasing the cost, to employers. There are both economic and social justifications for these reforms. Generous social systems can weaken economic growth and job creation by creating artificial shortages of low-skill labour and forcing up its cost, since employers have to bid against social-assistance payments.

The social justification is to halt the growth of dependent subpopulations and reduce the social problems related to dependence; to encourage youth to remain in educational and skill-enhancing streams rather than become another dependent generation; and, indirectly, to reduce long-term poverty. Pay rates are typically low for new labour-force entrants and for re-entrants into the labour market. Thus, social assistance can offer a higher level of living at this stage – and that's the reason for reducing perverse incentives, on one hand, and increasing take-home pay though tax cuts, on the other. But, in the longer term, pay progressively increases with work experience, as both skills and work discipline are gained. Thus, in the longer term, those who enter the labour market, even at initially low rates of pay, are likely to escape poverty, unlike those who remain on social assistance.

However, corporatist states may face a time-limit problem.

Corporatist states must depend on consensus between key players rather than automatic market mechanisms. As union leaders readily acknowledge in both Ireland and the Netherlands, only the dire economic conditions of the 1970s and 1980s brought home the need for wage restraint and an improved profit performance. Now that the economies of both nations are doing well and the labour market is tightening, there are signs the agreements are coming unraveled, with increasing numbers of union members voting against agreements negotiated by union leadership. In Ireland, fiscal restraint is weakening, and government expenditures are growing rapidly, though the strength of the economy continues to generate strong tax revenues, and the government's overall fiscal position is good.

The Netherlands, even more than Ireland, provides a study of the time-limited nature of corporatist recovery. That's because the Netherlands has been through the corporatist cycle several times and has experienced both the breakdown of social consensus and its rebuilding. The recent Irish society-wide wage and tax agreements are Ireland's first large-scale experiments with the corporatist strategy.

In the Netherlands, a strong social consensus between unions, business, and government, including a harmonious agreement on the need for wage restraint, following World War II led to a prolonged period of growth. Wage restraint came unravelled in the 1960s and 1970s. Good times, supplemented by natural-gas revenues, led to increasing government expenditures. But government's appetite was even greater. Both taxes and the deficit rose dramatically. Spending was out of control. This was classic "Dutch disease".

Through the 1970s, Dutch unemployment, which had been virtually non-existent, soared. Dutch GDP fell relative to other advanced economies, and the deficit rapidly rose. Dutch unions aggressively bargained for every cent they could get. But inflation wiped away gains, and the economy continued to deteriorate both for unionized and non-union workers. These circumstances led to a breakthrough social pact on wage restraint in 1982 and a return to growth. This began to come unravelled again in the early 1990s, after the economy had returned to a higher growth path. Renewed wage pressure dramatically weakened Dutch economic perform-ance in the early 1990s. This was enough to alarm the members of the social pact – labour, business, and government – back into an even stronger pact than before. This time the social partners added on a menu of significant government cuts and tax relief. This was under a new prime minister, Wim Kok, head of the La-bour Party and former leader of the Netherlands' largest union federation. Kok, as finance minister in the early 1990s, was re-sponsible for the first significant cuts in runaway welfare spend-ing. By the mid-1990s, growth has resumed. This is the period policy-makers and journalists have dubbed the "Dutch miracle".

The corporatist model faces another serious problem in the pricing of labour. Labour rates are determined not by market forces but by agreement between powerful corporate bodies. This is remarkably similar to the much greater problem the planned Soviet-style economies faced, and the solution is remarkably simi-lar. Economic policy-makers look to what is happening in other economies to set prices. The corporatist players in Ireland and the Netherlands look at labour costs in nearby nations and use this as a base, tacking on productivity improvements, currency fluctuations, and other adjustments.

TROUBLED ECONOMIES

As a point of comparison, Chapter 4 also looks at jurisdictions that have performed less well, Louisiana and Maine, though Maine boasts a somewhat more successful record.

Louisiana has long been a Southern laggard, yet it would seem better suited for economic growth than any other Southern state. It has a large population, creating a significant domestic market. It has the Deep South's largest city, New Orleans, which is situ-ated on one of the world's greatest trade routes, the Mississippi River.

Moreover, unlike the other Deep South states, Louisiana is blessed with immense resource wealth, huge petrochemical reserves.[14] Yet, more than other Southern states, Louisiana has a deeply politicized economy. This creates economic distortions, diverts resources from their most efficient uses, weakens government provision of real services, and creates a difficult climate for business. "Louisiana is the only southern state with a reputation for being hostile to business" (Holmes 1996, 29).

Perhaps the most telling episode in recent Louisiana economic history was the oil boom at the end of the 1970s. Because of the state's petrochemical wealth, state GDP skyrocketed as did state revenues. It was Louisiana's bout of "Dutch disease". Government grew larger, costs increased, and, unlike Texas and Alberta, the state did not use resource wealth to reduce taxes to offset the increased costs non-petrochemical businesses faced during the oil boom, as rich petrochemical companies bid up the price of labour, land, and materials. Survival became increasingly difficult for businesses that did not benefit from the petrochemical boom.

As a result, when the boom was over, Louisiana's economy nosedived. New non-petrochemical businesses had not been built, and existing businesses had been bloated and weakened by the boom. High levels of state spending through the boom did little to improve infrastructure or services. All informed observers I spoke with in Louisiana – from economists to senior government officials – believed the money had been squandered by the state government. They pointed to lack of infrastructure improvements to support this view. In the end, both the petrochemical industry and government activity increased costs through the Louisiana economy without offsetting these costs through tax reductions or useful government expenditures. This crowded out other activities and left the Louisiana economy devastated when the oil boom busted.

Maine, too, has underperformed the convergence effect. The state has long suffered from unusually high taxes by U.S. stand-

---

14. The phrase "blessed with" should be read ironically because resource wealth is too often a curse. Natural gas was the root cause of "Dutch disease" and resource-rich nations in general tend to grow more slowly than less endowed nations.

ards. Nonetheless, Maine has grown much more strongly than the neighouring Atlantic Canadian provinces, whose per capita GDP continues to fall further and further behind per capita GDP in Maine. Moreover, there are more recent signs Maine's economic vigour is increasing. As well, a new administration elected in the mid-1990s is directly tackling costs and attempting to make the state more responsive to business. It will be interesting to watch the results from this effort.

Chapter 2
The Celtic Tiger

The harder you work, the luckier you get.
Gary Player

INTRODUCTION AND OVERVIEW

Ireland has been one of the globe's uncontested economic stars since 1987, when a new fiscally responsible, tax-cutting government was elected to office, and a society-wide agreement was struck to hold down labour costs. Ireland may now be the world's brightest star. Until a few years ago, the Asian tigers would have held equal claim to pre-eminent status, but Ireland has suffered none of their economic set-backs. Economic growth has accelerated, even as other parts of the world suffered economic turmoil and during a period when most of Ireland's European trading partners were mired in sluggish growth or recession.

Irish policy-makers regard tax cuts and wage moderation – explicitly designed to reduce costs in the Irish economy and to increase profits – as the corner-stones of recent Irish success. The 1987–88 reforms came at a fortuitous time, a time of real opportunity for the Emerald Isle, but then, as Gary Player might have said, "The better your policies, the luckier you get." Ireland in the late 1980s and the 1990s was able to take advantage of economic opportunities, whereas before it had missed or destroyed opportunity. Until the late 1980s, the question that outside observers asked had not been, as it is now, "How do we copy Ireland's success?" but rather "Why is Ireland forever destined to remain a have-not region, lagging its neighbours?" Ireland suffered deep economic gloom through most of the 1980s.

This sense of foreboding and an understanding of the disastrous mix of policies Ireland developed through the 1970s and

1980s led to the political will needed to carry through fundamental reforms. These reforms cut costs in the Irish economy and made it a profitable place to do business and invest, leading to unprecedented wealth creation and job generation in recent years. Ireland's economic record through to 1987 was dismal and in part a hangover from the 1970s. Irish governments had steadily increased the public debt through the 1970s, and things were getting worse. In 1977, Ireland elected a government which claimed it could spend its way out of economic stagnation. Between 1974 and 1986, the deficit was over 10 per cent of GDP for all but two years. In 1982, it exceeded 14 per cent of GDP. Yet, despite all this government spending, employment growth was stagnant at best, and all too often negative. Even though Ireland had a high birth rate, the total number of jobs in 1986 was virtually identical to the number in 1971, and there were fewer jobs in industry. In real terms, the Irish economy grew by less than 1.5 per cent on average from 1980 to 1986, less than a third of the preceding rate and less than a quarter of the rate of growth since. Thousands of young Irish left their home country.

The magnitude of the turn-around is hard to grasp. Prior to 1986, Ireland had experienced years of zero job growth and job losses in the industrial sector. But, by 1996, Ireland had one-fifth more jobs than in 1986. Even more remarkably, the number of industrial jobs increased by one-third. More jobs were generated in just three years – a 12 per cent increase between 1993 and 1996 – than in the preceding 30 years (OECD 1997a, 25).

Although employment growth had until recently been one of the weaker aspects of the Irish turn-around, growth in Irish employment has outpaced both the OECD average and the EU average since the mid-1990s. More remarkably, recent Irish employment growth has even outpaced the exceptional rate of job growth in United States (ESRI 1997a, 36). In Ireland, the employment rate – the ratio of employment to the total labour force – rose by 2.2 percentage points between 1991 and 1996. In the other EU-15 nations, it fell on average by 0.7 percentage points (Sachs 1997, 54). From 1995 to 1997, over 50,000 additional jobs were generated each year. Nearly 100,000 jobs were created in 1998. In 1999, unemployment fell to under 6 per cent, down from 17 per cent in 1987.

Ireland's economic growth has been even more spectacular than its stellar record of job creation. Ireland's GDP has achieved real average growth of over 6 per cent since 1986 and over 7 per cent since 1994. In 1997, it was nearly 11 per cent and in 1998 nearly 9 per cent.

In direct contradiction to the old Keynesian assumptions, this was accomplished during a period, of sometimes intense government retrenchment. This was particularly true at the beginning of the period, when spending cuts actually seemed to spark new growth. Despite large cuts in taxation, the deficit has been slashed, and the debt–to–GDP ratio has steadily declined, as GDP growth responded to tax cuts and wage moderation. Thousands of Irish expatriates are returning, and, for the first time in modern history, Ireland is experiencing a *sustained* net inward immigration. The change in the Irish economy has been truly remarkable: "As late as 1961, Ireland was a backward, poor, agricultural region of the UK economy. Today it is a developed, industrial region of the European economy" (Baker 1997, 3).

What happened? The Irish focused on costs in the economy. The government reduced the costs under its control, steadily cutting taxes since 1987 and lessening the uncertainty costs related to large deficits. These factors alone have made Ireland a more attractive place to invest, both for foreigners and for the Irish themselves. Moreover, the bad years of the 1980s had produced a society-wide consensus that Ireland had to be made more competitive and that profits needed to be boosted.

This was a view shared by the union leadership. In 1987, unions, business, and government negotiated the first of a series of agreements designed to moderate wage increases. This controlled another key cost in the economy, the cost of labour. What the unions wanted in return provided even more stimulus to economic growth and job creation. They wanted further tax cuts so that, given the agreements on wage moderation, their members could take home more of their pay and government would take less. After-tax real income has grown strongly since, despite moderate wage increases. Finally, fiscal restraint and wage moderation slashed inflation. This reduces costs related to inflation, most notably the cost of uncertainty.

Yet trouble may already be brewing. With the good times, the social consensus could come unravelled. Hard times forged hard decisions. The various sectors of the economy may no longer be satisfied with the same proportion of an ever larger pie, but may want a bigger share, too. If this results in increasing costs that cut into Ireland's high profit levels; the golden goose, discussed earlier, may be headed for the chopping block.

A HISTORY OF ECOMONIC WEAKNESS

In any society, a bloody upheaval reduces living standards in its aftermath. This was true of the American, French, both Russian revolutions, and countless others. It was certainly true of Ireland in the 1920s, following a bloody war of independence and then a similarly bloody civil war. As the violence wound down, economic times were grim under the government of William Cosgrove, 1922 to 1932. Cosgrove aimed for an open economy and fiscal prudence. While a few economists detect some economic improvement under the Cosgrove government, if it did exist, it wasn't enough.

Éamon de Valera assumed power in 1932. His plan was to generate growth domestically. Tariff walls were thrown up. Import substitution would generate jobs and economic growth. The policy was an utter failure, as Jeffrey Sachs notes:

> The most famous phase in modern [Irish economic] history was 1932–57, when Ireland launched a policy of import substituting industrialization in the depths of the Depression. The notoriety of Ireland's policy was magnified by John Maynard Keynes' endorsement of the inward-looking strategy in his famous Finlay Lecture on "Economic self-sufficiency" delivered at University

College, Dublin, in April 1933. The policy in retrospect was a debacle. (Sachs 1997, 58)[1]

The imposition of this inward-looking policy brought what weak economic growth there was to a stuttering halt in the 1930s, but it would be hardly fair to draw conclusions from Ireland's performance during the extraordinary Depression or war years.

The closed-door policy remained in effect in the post-war years, and here is where it is possible to take a measure of the impact of this policy. Despite powerful economic growth in Britain, Europe, and North America, in Ireland,

> [r]eal national income virtually stagnated between 1950 and 1958 ... A corrosive pessimism took over. The July 1956 issue of the satirical monthly, *Dublin Opinion,* bore a cartoon on its cover showing a map of Ireland with the caption "Shortly Available Underdeveloped Country ... Owners Going Abroad. ..." It was only when the rest of Europe left the Irish economy standing in the 1950s that the bankruptcy of the old policies became clear to policy makers. (Ó Gráda 1997, 27 and 49)

Ireland, with its closed-door trade policy, had the slowest growth in all of Europe through the 1950s, even as other, more-damaged nations were rapidly rebuilding their economies. Thousands of people were leaving Ireland to seek work in Britain, the United States, and other English-speaking nations.

Then, Irish policy abruptly changed in the late 1950s. The closed Irish economy was opened. Strong economic growth appeared for the first time in modern Irish history. Ireland had entered its first golden age of growth.

---

1. Sachs notes that this flew in the face of Keynes's otherwise strong support for free trade.

The First Golden Age

A couple of curiosities surround Ireland's first golden age of economic growth. The central puzzle relates to the magnitude of the turn-around. The only deep policy change was the move from a closed economy to an open economy. Ireland through the 1950s had been fiscally responsible. The move to an open economy certainly boosted economic activity. Through the 1960s, exports grew by nearly 7 per cent a year in real terms and industrial production by over 6 per cent. Yet many economists have been reluctant to attribute Ireland's astounding turn-around – from virtually zero growth to about 4 per cent a year – solely to this one policy change.[2]

However, Sachs (1997) notes the shift to an open-door policy was also accompanied by important cuts in corporate taxes, which attracted a strong inflow of foreign investment for the first time in recent Irish history. And Arrow (1997, 7) discusses how an open economy spurs competitiveness and efficiency through a small economy: "In a small country, it can easily happen that there are too few firms in an industry to permit adequate competition; foreign competition is needed. Competition is important partly to reduce markups and therefore increase consumer welfare but even more importantly to create a steady pressure for efficiency."

The other curiosity is that Seán Lemass, the architect of De Valera's protection policy, engineered this reverse course. Lemass was "determined to overturn the very policies with which he had been identified since the 1930s" (Ó Gráda 1997, 29).

The result was a "fundamental policy change ... in the '60s, gradually moving away from protection to an open export-based economy, with diversification away from the UK market. Membership in the EU from 1973 played a vital role in this modernizing process" (Baker 1997, 3).

In short, Ireland in its first golden age had a policy regime with many elements very similar to the policy regime credited with the nation's growth in the 1990s, in particular a fiscally responsible

---

2. Recent research, however, shows powerful positive economic effects from openness. See, for example, Sachs and Warner (1995).

government and an open economy. GDP growth was strong (charts 2-1 and 2-2). But this would change.

The Bad Years and Their Prelude

Ireland, like other industrial nations, suffered a set-back with the oil crisis in late 1973. Government responded in Ireland, as it did elsewhere, with increased spending and ever-larger deficits. The economy was well into recovery by 1975, yet the government continued to spend. Deficits averaged around 10 per cent of GDP, and then they got worse (chart 2-3).

In 1977, a new government, led by Jack Lynch, was elected by a landslide. Ireland's fiscal position was already perilous, but Lynch's Fianna Fáil's "extravagant and irresponsible election programme" (Ó Gráda 1997, 31) promised to spend the nation's way to new economic growth. By the early 1980s, the deficit had soared to more than 14 per cent of GDP. This is a period which virtually all Irish commentators now regard with something near horror:[3]

> The 1979-87 period is recalled as one of very poor economic performance on almost all counts: slow growth, rapidly deteriorating public finances, stagnation of per capita disposable income, huge imbalances of payments, deficits and industrial relations turmoil. (NESC 1996, 9)

Although Irish growth was strong through the late 1970s, when large deficits began to develop, Irish economic analysts draw a direct link to the following period of weak growth:

> [I]nitially [government fiscal stimulus] had every appearance of success, with rapid economic growth, a reduction in the unemployment rate (to 7.2 per cent in 1979), and significant net immigration [though short-lived] for the first time in a generation. The costs came with a lag. The government had to borrow heavily, and so the ratio of

---

3. See, for example, Tansey (1998), Ó Gráda (1997), Haughton (1995), and Sachs (1997). This is also the sense I had in interviews with Irish officials in the spring of 1998.

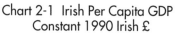

Chart 2-1 Irish Per Capita GDP
Constant 1990 Irish £

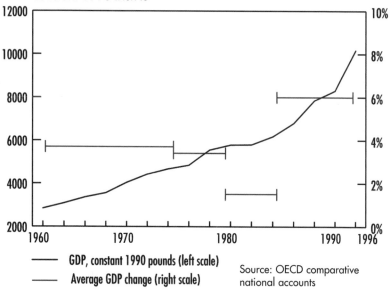

——— GDP, constant 1990 pounds (left scale)
——— Average GDP change (right scale)

Source: OECD comparative
national accounts

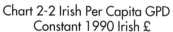

Chart 2-2 Irish Per Capita GPD
Constant 1990 Irish £

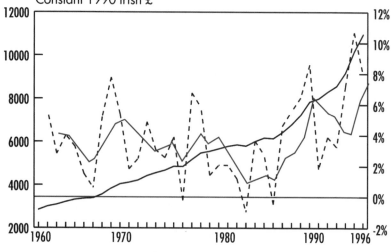

——— GDP, constant 1990 Irish pounds (left scale)
- - - - Annual change (right scale)
——— 4 per. Mov. Avg. (annual change: right scale)

Source: OECD comparative
national accounts

Chart 2-3   Irish Budget Deficit Including Grants (% of GDP)

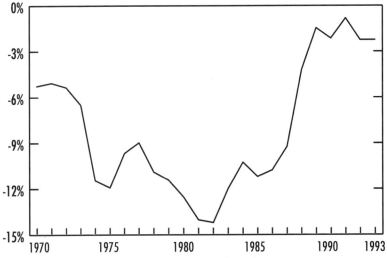

Source: World Development Indicators 1997: World Bank

debt to GDP rose, from 52 per cent in 1973 to 129 per cent by 1987, by then easily the highest in the European Union. By 1986, the cost of servicing this debt took up 94 per cent of all revenue from personal income tax. Successive governments initially tried to solve the problem by raising tax rates, especially in 1981 and 1983, but these changes hardly increased tax revenue, suggesting that the country was close to its revenue maximising tax rates. (Haughton 1995, 39)

Irish average economic growth from the mid-1970s to the latter part of the decade was only a shade lower than the growth through the post-1958 period, but it came at the cost of unsustainable imbalances, which would lead to the prolonged downturn. Growth weakened in the late 1970s and often turned negative in the 1980s. "The imbalances that accompanied the growth of the period 1976–81 are quite striking when compared to the balanced nature of the growth performance since the mid-1980s" (ESRI 1997a, 38). (See chart 2-4, which reproduces ESRI, 39.)

Chart 2-4 Growth, Inflation, EBR and BoP as Share of GNP of
(a) 1976-81 and (b) 1987-96 — ESA 79 Basis

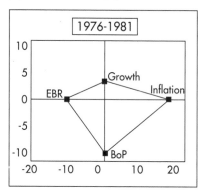 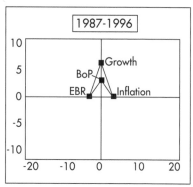

Nonetheless, the government continued to promise new growth through Keynesian techniques. Deficits were kept high, and this fiscal stimulus was to generate new growth:

> Never before or since has an Irish government got it so wrong. The slow growth — the economy would contract by 0.5 per cent in 1982 — put paid to "revenue buoyancy" [the predicted Keynesian stimulus which would solve the fiscal problems] and high interest rates added to the public debt burden. At the time, both the deficit and the rise in PSBR [Public Sector Borrowing Requirement] were rationalized in Keynesian terms. But budget deficits continued to accumulate in the following few years ... raising the PSBR and national debt to clearly unsustainable levels. (Ó Gráda 1997, 70-71)

Both skyrocketing deficits and increasing large government expenditures had a negative impact on growth, through the "crowding out" effect:

> [T]here is the added consideration that fiscal policy may "crowd out" private sector investment. This conclusion would appear to be borne out by the Irish experience.

Between 1972 and 1987 fiscal policy in Ireland led to a significant increase in the national debt without having the desired effect on growth and employment. (Leddin & O'Leary 1995, 194)

The "crowding out" effect occurs through several channels. Large government borrowing forces up the cost of capital, making investment more expensive. High taxes reduce the money people and businesses have to spend and invest. Government expenditures bid up the cost of scarce resources – labour, land, and supplies – again making investment more expensive. And high taxes coupled with generous social programmes create incentive not to work, furthering inflating the cost of labour.

Along with Ireland's deteriorating fiscal position, labour problems were serious. Unions rapidly pushed up wages. Unit labour costs in particular soared. Yet real wages shrank. High taxes and union militancy had virtually eliminated profits, thereby destroying the incentive and the means for further investment. The productivity of the Irish economy deteriorated. Thus, there was simply less pie to share, and that had inevitable consequences for real wages, no matter how high the nominal settlements.

Falling real wages fed back into increasing labour strife. In 1979, more than 1.4 million days were lost to labour disputes. That deepened the economic troubles. The economy shed tens of thousands of jobs. Unemployment would have been far worse had not many thousands chosen to emigrate.

Export growth was essentially flat between 1977 and 1982, but grew thereafter (chart 2-5). But growth between 1982 and 1987 was largely due to weakness in the domestic market. The domestic weakness is, of course, evident in a broad range of economic figures, and it is also reflected in the fact that net exports grew even more rapidly than exports through this period. After 1987, export growth was more balanced.

This period also bequeathed to Ireland a new problem, one that still persists – urban ghettos largely occupied by long-term unemployed (OECD, 1997a, 58-74). Because of the escape valve

Chart 2-5   Irish Exports of Goods and Services (% of GDP)

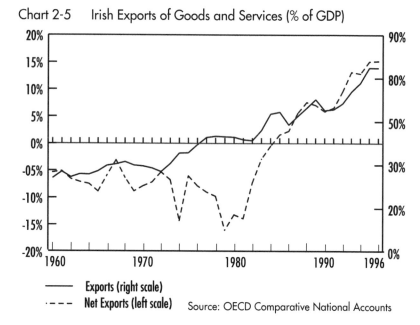

——— Exports (right scale)
· – – – Net Exports (left scale)   Source: OECD Comparative National Accounts

of emigration, even in bad times, Ireland seldom had a high unemployment rate. But, through the 1970s and early 1980s, the government increased personal transfer payments while also boosting personal taxes. The combination of the two made it more profitable for many to collect social payments than to work or emigrate.[4]

The difference between unemployment as measured by the Labour Force Survey (LFS) and the Live Register Unemployment (LRU), essentially those claiming benefits, gives some indication of the number of beneficiaries who were simply not willing to look for or accept work. The LFS is a survey asking people if they are willing to accept work and looking for it; in other words, whether they were unemployed by the official measure. The LRU is simply the count of the number of people claiming unemployment benefits.

---

4. These problems are discussed in Burda (1997, 95-109) and, more extensively, throughout Tansey (1998).

Chart 2-6 Unemployment Measures ('000s)

— Labour Force Survey - - - - Live Register Unemployment —— Difference

Source: Tansey (1998, 92)

For some years, the number of people collecting unemployment benefits exceeded the number of people officially unemployed in Ireland. In 1995, according to the OECD (1997a, 69), the number of people collecting benefits was 50 per cent higher than the unemployment rate (chart 2-6). The widening gap between the two in recent years reflects the increasing availability of jobs in Ireland for those seeking employment. Thus, almost anyone who has wanted a job could find one, lowering the rate of unemployment but little affecting the number of those content to collect benefits.

Of course, Ireland is not unique in this. In many jurisdictions, the number of people collecting unemployment benefits exceeds the number of people officially unemployed. This is true in many European nations, and spectacularly true in Atlantic Canada, where the number of people collecting unemployment was often twice as high as the official number of unemployed (see McMahon 2000). The long-term nature of much of Ireland's unemployment again reveals a class of unemployed with little connection to the labour market. The OECD (1997, 177) found that about 60 per cent of Ireland's unemployed were long-term unemployed.

"There are whole areas of this city where there is no culture of employment," Manus O'Riordan, head of research for Ireland's largest union association, the Services Industrial Professional Union, told me while I was in Dublin in June 1998. The creation of the "no-employment" culture occurred in just one generation. As earlier noted, unemployment was virtually non-existent in Ireland prior to the 1970s because of the safety valve of emigration in weak economic times. O'Riordan and the union movement do not support a reduction in social payments, but they are vocally calling for further tax reduction. "Taxes are a disincentive to work. We need incentives to work," O'Riordan says. Nonetheless, at that time the Irish government was pushing to reform social payments, to make them less generous and harder to obtain, particularly for younger workers. The government hoped to avoid trapping another generation in the culture of the dole, a sentiment shared by O'Riordan, though he would prefer to work with incentives through the tax code.

I got a first-hand sense of the gloom which had descended over Ireland between 1980 and 1986 in a conversation in the Central Bank of Ireland's disconcertingly modern building in the heart of historic Dublin. I had asked about the early 1980s. Hugh O'Donnell, the bank's chief spokesman, visibly sighed. "Those were dreary times, weren't they, Rafique?" he asked his colleague Rafique Mottiar, a senior bank economist and Irishman for the past 25 years. "We had thought emigration was a problem of the past," O'Donnell continued, "but thousands of people were leaving each year." Mottiar turned to me and added, "It seemed half the college graduating class went straight from graduating ceremonies to the airport, for America." Ireland had become a high-cost place to do business, troubled by militant unions and high taxes, and suffering from private-sector crowding out due to big government, large deficits, and the resulting impact on interest rates.

In a separate conversation, O'Riordan said much the same thing as O'Donnell and Mottiar: "We had declining economic growth and declining employment. Wages were up, but inflation and taxes were up more. Living standards were declining. We knew we had to do something."

However, the doom-and-gloom sense of the time may have had positive benefits in line with the earlier discussion of the nature of reform in a corporatist economy. "This perceived failure of economic policy undoubtedly added to the mood of pessimism which pervaded the public debate at the time. However this air of desperation, particularly concerning employment prospects, itself engendered a profound shift in attitudes which laid the foundation for the subsequent sustained recovery" (ESRI 1997a, 63).

DOING SOMETHING

For most of the post-independence period, Ireland either had a fiscally prudent government (virtually the entire period from independence to the 1970s) or an open economy (the period after 1958). Prior to 1987, they overlapped only in the period from the late 1950s to the first oil shock, the first period of strong Irish economic growth. They were to be reunited in the late 1980s. Two further policy initiatives were added – a social contract explicitly designed to moderate labour costs and increase profits, and a commitment to tax reductions. We'll look at government cuts first and then consider the labour situation.

Fiscal Reform

Although the 1987 election resulted in a minority government, a broad consensus had developed that the public finances had to be put in order. The new government under Charles Haughey acted quickly. Two days after being appointed finance minister, Ray McSharry – soon nicknamed Mac-the-knife – killed a planned pay raise for senior civil servants. This was a small foretaste of what was to come. Reflecting the society-wide consensus, these reforms were continued when Haughey's Fianna Fáil was replaced in government in 1994 by the "Rainbow coalition" of parties including, Fine Gael, Labour, and Democratic Left. The coalition was headed by Fine Gael leader John Bruton, who became president of the EU Council in 1996.[5]

The cuts were, if anything, more severe than those made in Margaret Thatcher's Britain or Ronald Reagan's United States. By 1989, two years after the election, government spending was lower as a percentage of GDP than in 1979. Remarkably, government spending fell from an average of over half of GDP between 1982 and 1987 to around 40 per cent of GDP in 1989 (charts 2-7 and 2-8). This was a much larger and much quicker cut of government as a per cent of GDP than Thatcher had engineered almost a decade earlier in Great Britain. This holds true as well when averaged over years rather than measured from peaks to troughs. In comparing the periods 1980–1984 and 1990–1994, government spending in Ireland declined by 5 per cent of GDP, compared to 2.3 per cent of GDP in Britain (de la Fuente & Vives 1997, 104).

Keynesian economics would predict disastrous results for a retrenchment or negative fiscal stimulus this abrupt and large, particularly when an economy already was in recession. Economic growth had been negative in 1986. It would seem cut-backs could not have come a worse time, just when the economy needed stimulus, not restrictive policies. Even the advocates of fiscal retrenchment expected economic turmoil and economic weakness during an adjustment period. What happened surprised everyone, no matter how optimistic or supportive of Haughey's policy.

Economic growth took off immediately with the budget cuts. Negative in 1986, it was transformed to a positive growth ratio of 4.5 per cent in 1987, the year of the cuts. This was the strongest growth since 1977. But things got even better. Growth steadily rose to over 8.5 per cent in 1990, the strongest yearly growth Ireland had yet achieved in its history. For the first three years of the 1990s, growth fell back to 2 to 4 per cent before ratcheting up to more than 7 per cent for the next years of the 1990s, including over 10 per cent growth in 1995. Sounder fiscal policies, combined with a

---

5. Bruton may be even better known for his social reforms, including the removal of Ireland's ban on divorce.

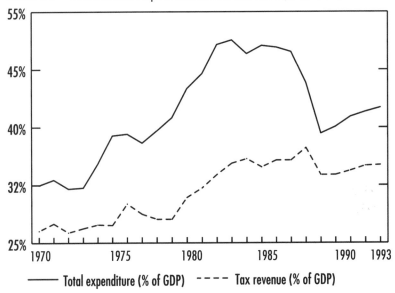

Chart 2-7   Government Expenditures and Revenue (% of GDP)

—— Total expenditure (% of GDP)   - - - - Tax revenue (% of GDP)

Source: World Development Indicators 1997: World Bank

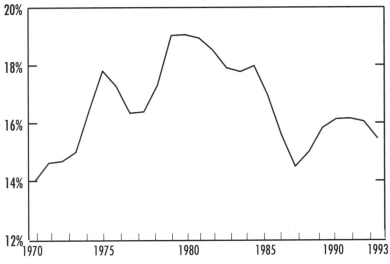

Chart 2-8 Irish Government Consumption (% of GDP)

Source: World Development Indicators 1997: World Bank

change in attitude and a growing commitment to wage moderation, seemed to have powered the growth. "The bipartisan commitment to putting public finances in order had apparently restored the confidence of both consumers and private investors" (Ó Gráda 1997, 32).

Economists began to speculate about "expansionary fiscal contraction", or EFC. The apparently contradictory phrase is meant to capture the idea that government activities distort the economy and crowd out other activity. Therefore a lessening of government activity can stimulate, rather than retard, growth. The NESC (1996, 24-25) discusses

> the tendency for various government incentives to produce rent-seeking financial manipulation, rather than increased business initiative. ... Failures seem to have arisen – in periods of both growth or recession – when there was insufficient recognition that the cost and effectiveness of the public sector impacted strongly on the competitiveness of, and the burdens on, the private sector.[6]

De la Fuente and Vives (1997, 124-125) also discuss the reductions in economic distortions to which government retrenchment can lead. Their econometric estimates show a large positive impact from government cut-backs:

> Tax and expenditure reductions can be expected to increase growth by reducing disincentives that tend to depress investment and labor supply. King and Rebelo, 1990, show the impact of these effects can be quite important, especially in the case of a small open economy. Since we are controlling for both employment and factor accumulation, however, our [econometric] estimates are presumably not picking up these effects, or the 'crowding out' of private investment, but a negative externality effect of

---

6. This discussion is not explicitly tied to the EFC idea, but it covers similar territory.

government size on the efficiency of resource allocation and on work effort ... [O]ur results are consistent with the view that fiscal adjustment [contraction] was directly responsible for a sizable increase in [Ireland's] growth rate.[7]

EFC is also meant to capture the impact of the confidence-building nature of fiscal responsibility and the resulting expectation of lower taxes. Lower taxes increase after-tax incomes and increase incentives to work, boosting growth. Increases in consumption related to greater income further spur economic growth. Most importantly, the promise of lower taxes, and thus higher profits, could serve as a magnet for investment.

Yet the situation was not quite so simple. The evidence is convincing that reforms designed to redress deficits through expenditure cut-backs produce long-term benefits. For example, Alesina and Perotti (1995) survey OECD nations which attempted to re-establish fiscal balance. They find that nations, which do this through expenditure cuts achieve significantly better results than nations which tackle deficits through tax increases.[8] Alesina and Perotti measure success through debt- and deficit-to-GDP ratios. Most interestingly, a large part of the difference between the two groups of countries is stronger GDP growth in the first group.

But economic adjustment is not instantaneous, and a government retrenchment as large as Ireland's should have created short-term dislocations in the period immediately following the cut-backs before renewed private-sector activity crowded in. But policymakers had the luck of the Irish in their timing. The Irish pound had been devalued in 1986, making Irish exports more price-competitive. In the long term, devaluation is no way to save an

---

7. King and Rebelo (1990) is cited as a reference for this book. De la Fuente and Vives also cite (p.124) a number of other works which support the idea of an EFC, though they do not use the term.

8. Tax increases in Canada, mainly bracket creep due to lack of indexation of income-tax rates, have carried the weight of about two-thirds of Canada's deficit fight. Canada's relatively weak economic performance through this period appears consistent with Alesina and Perotti's results.

economy. It simply indicates falling productivity compared to that in other nations, and implies that economic reforms are needed to improve productivity growth. But it can provide a temporary boost, and this helped Ireland, which was on the verge of fundamental reform.

The devaluation of the Irish pound was coupled with a fall in international interest rates, which promoted investment and helped lead to unexpectedly strong world-wide growth. Growth in the United Kingdom was also strong, due to large tax cuts in that country. These factors combined to strengthen export growth and encourage private-sector investment, just as government was cutting back.

Nonetheless, the EFC hypothesis does capture real economic phenomena. Barry and Devereux (1995) modelled the EFC hypotheses and found that forward-looking behaviour – based on the expectation of tax cuts – would partly offset a fiscal contraction in the short term before new, longer-term growth was sparked by the cuts. But this offset is only partial. More interestingly, they found forward-looking behaviour, when coupled with the positive external shocks, could in fact lead to a result similar to EFC. Moreover, in the long term, government efficiency and taxation levels have a large impact on economic growth:

> [I]t should be recognized that the performance of government is an important determinant of international competitiveness. An efficient government enhances the ability of domestic firms to compete in international markets, by reducing the taxation, and other costs of obtaining policy objectives. (In international empirical studies, an efficient government is highly correlated with strong economic performance ...) (Lane 1995, 125; bracketed comments in the original)

Reforms stabilized Ireland's fiscal environment, reducing the costs associated with uncertainty, costs related to inflation as well as forward-looking concerns about taxes:

Research suggests ... a stable macroeconomic environment is also a key element of economic growth. This has important implications for attempts to assess the growth performance of the Irish economy over the past three decades since it implies that the severe macroeconomic imbalances of the early 1980s may have contributed directly to the poor growth performance at that time. (ESRI 1997a, 46)

One other important fact emerges from a consideration of Ireland's recent fiscal history. Cutting taxes, far from being a race to the bottom in government services, instead soon increases government revenues through the cut's impact on economic growth. This is true in most jurisdictions which have initiated significant tax cuts, and it is certainly true of the Irish experience. Revenues fell in 1988, immediately after the cuts, but within a year, by 1989, inflation-adjusted tax revenues exceeded the revenues received by government prior to the tax cuts (chart 2-9).

Wage Moderation

As important as fiscal reform was, even more important was a trilateral agreement between government, unions, and business to hold wage growth down and increase profits, and thus boost the attractiveness of Ireland for investment.

The three-year *Programme for National Recovery* (PNR) agreement signed in October 1987 embodied the concepts of labour peace and pay moderation in exchange for tax cuts, as discussed earlier. It has been followed by successive agreements, most recently *Partnership 2000*, which commits the government to further tax reductions. The tax cuts under these programmes have been substantial. For instance, the PNR explicitly targeted tax reductions of £225 million but the cuts were later calculated to have totalled £800 million (Tansey 1998, 147). Using the exchange rates of the time, the saving roughly equalled $1.6 billion Canadian or $1.25 billion U.S., a significant reduction for a nation of about 3.5 million people. As well, the agreements specifically

Chart 2-9   Irish Tax Revenues in Real Terms (1987 = 100)

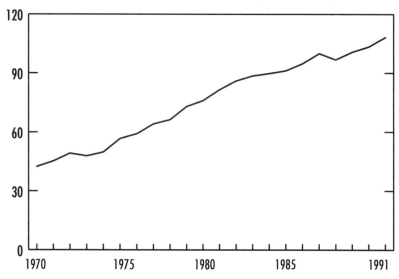

recognized the competitive boost and job-generating impact of moderate wage growth.

Wage increases in Ireland had actually been slowing for some time prior to 1987 (chart 2-10). Nominal increases in the manufacturing wage had hit a high of over 25 per cent in the inflationary years following the first oil shock. They continued to range of between 15 and 20 per cent a year until the early 1980s. In 1984, wage increases dipped below 10 per cent and slid slightly through to 1986. In 1987, wage increases dropped below 5 per cent and then stayed in the range of 5 per cent until 1993, when they fell well below 5 per cent in spite of Ireland's astonishing growth in these years.

The OECD (1997a, 93) suggests the agreements may have had less direct impact on wage moderation than might be thought. It notes that the two most important factors in wage determination are inflation and after-tax income. The fiscal restructuring helped bring inflation down and created an expectation of lower taxes. The explicit promise of tax reductions in the PNR and later agree-

Chart 2-10   Hourly Earnings and Inflation (1992=100)

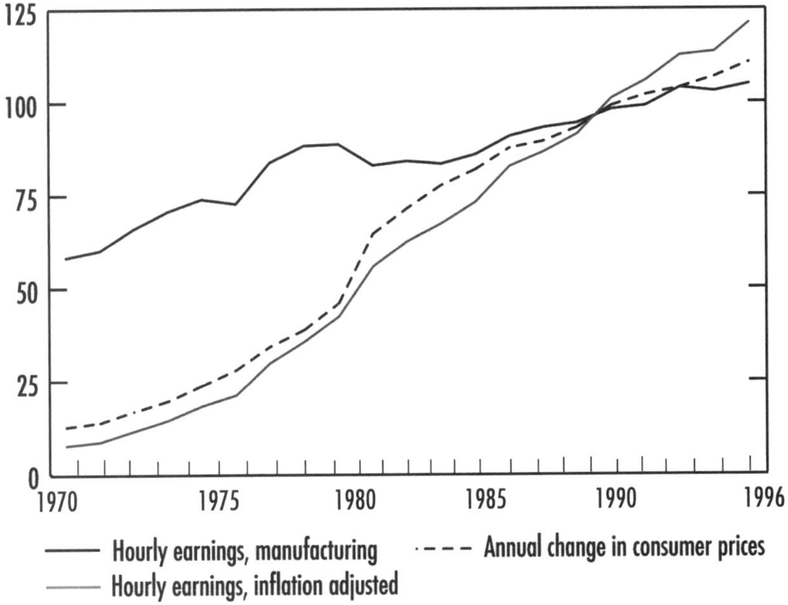

Hourly earnings, manufacturing   ·– – – Annual change in consumer prices
Hourly earnings, inflation adjusted

Source: OECD Main Economic Indicators

ments certainly added weight to this expectation. Of course, nominal wages are highly correlated to inflation, which fell from an annual rate of over 20 per cent in 1981 to about 2 per cent in 1988 (chart 2-11).

A number of factors clearly contributed to slower Irish wage growth. Although the PNR may have had less impact than meets the eye for the initial move to wage moderation, it and succeeding agreements have been crucial in maintaining low wage costs through Ireland's period of astounding growth.

Now we move to the central aspect of the wage story, which is neither nominal nor real wages but rather unit labour costs. ULCs are the true cost to business of labour. They take into account wages, inflation, and productivity growth. This reflects the real cost of labour per unit of output and is thus far more revealing than either nominal or even real wages.

Chart 2-11   Consumer Price Index (1990 = 100)

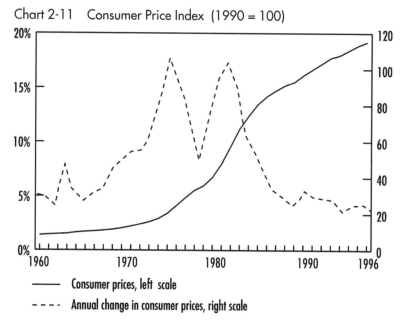

—— Consumer prices, left scale

- - - - Annual change in consumer prices, right scale

Source: OECD Main Economic Indicators

Stable prices and a commitment to moderate wage increases had a dramatic effect on ULCs. I provide two measures of ULC in manufacturing: one based on OECD wage numbers, and the other on the United States Bureau of Labor Statistics total hourly compensation costs. Total employment is multiplied by average weekly hours and real wage (or total compensation costs) and this is then divided by real manufacturing output.[9]

The results are similar for both series (charts 2-12 and 2-13). I will discuss the numbers produced using total compensation, as this gives a more complete picture of costs. Using an index where

---

9. The OECD average weekly hours used in this calculation is for the economy as a whole but should serve as a good proxy for changes in weekly manufacturing hours. Assuming a constant number of average weekly hours does not dramatically change the calculations, which are consistent with other work. For example, see OECD (1997a) calculations.

Chart 2-12 Unit Labour Costs and Wages: Manufacturing (1990 = 100)

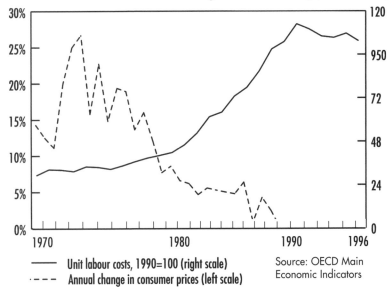

——— Unit labour costs, 1990=100 (right scale)
· - - - Annual change in consumer prices (left scale)

Source: OECD Main
Economic Indicators

Chart 2-13 Unit Labour Costs and Compensation: Manufacturing (1990 = 100)

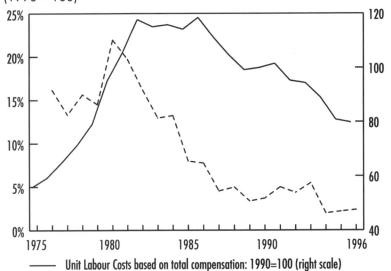

——— Unit Labour Costs based on total compensation: 1990=100 (right scale)
· - - - Annual change in nominal manufacturing total compensation (left scale)

Estimate of ULC: (real compensation x Hours x employees) /real output

Source: OECD Main Economic Indicators except hourly compensation from US Bureau of Labour Statistics, international comparisons of hourly compensation costs for production workers in manufacturing 1975-77

1990 = 100, ULC peaked in 1986 at 118, following a dramatic rise through the 1970s, which severely retarded Ireland's competitiveness. Following the *Programme for National Recovery* agreement, ULCs declined dramatically, clearly boosting Ireland's competitiveness. From 1988 to 1989, they declined by one-sixth, then after 1991 the index declined another 20 per cent, from just over 100 to just under 80. The relatively low price of labour also favoured job creation over other sorts of investment, as Krugman (1997, 42-43) notes:

> Given the combination of good productivity growth and wage constraint, the success of the economy is in a macro sense not hard to explain. With labor relatively inexpensive, the incentives were in place both for high rates of investment and for those investors to choose employment-creating rather than labor-saving techniques of production – a sharp contrast to what was happening in continental Europe. Also, given the depressed state of the European economy (especially since 1991), Ireland's steady decline in relative unit labour costs has amounted to a de facto devaluation, making its exports increasingly competitive and therefore stimulating demand for Irish products at a time when demand elsewhere in Europe was stagnant.

A key part of this story is the impact on labour of a change of attitude on the part of unions. From the late 1960s to the mid-1980s, the number of industrial disputes had fluctuated around 150 per year, peaking at over 250 in 1974 and again at nearly 200 in 1984 (NESC 1996, 13). Just as wage increases began to fall before the 1987 agreement, so too did industrial disputes, a trend which deepened after the agreement. By 1989, the number of disputes was less than 50, and it has stayed in that range since. The number of days lost to labour disputes tells the same story. Between 1976 and 1986, 546,000 days a year were lost to industrial disputes; between 1987 and 1996, only 121,000 days on average

Chart 2-14   Days Lost to Industrial Disputes ('000s)

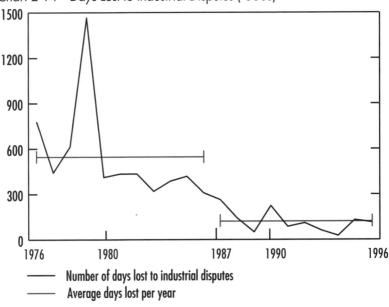

Source: Tansey (1998)

were lost each year to industrial action, well less than a quarter of the previous rate (see Tansey 1998, 156; and chart 2-14). Labour peace obviously reduces costs to business.

> Perhaps the most notable shift in attitudes was among the trade union leadership. In adopting a far more long-term perspective than had been common previously, they eased the way of adaptation to change in large sections of the economy, buttressed competitiveness by agreeing to moderate increases in nominal pay, with the beneficial side-effect of a sharp fall in days lost to industrial action, and, by becoming partners in a series of national agreements, broadened the consensus in favour of continuous fiscal responsibility. (ESRI 1997a, 64)

Labour-market Regulation

Efficient, well-functioning labour markets are also a key to keeping costs low in the economy. Ireland's corporatist model gives corporatist actors large influence in setting wages. Yet, as Sachs (1997, 61) notes, in other aspects, Ireland's labour markets are relatively free. Discussing an executive survey carried out by the World Economic Forum (WEF), Sachs writes: "Ireland's labour market regulations are *not* seen as seriously impeding the adjustment of labor hours to fluctuations in demand, at least in comparison to other European countries" (emphasis in the original).

Burda (1997) reaches the same conclusion. While Irish labour markets are not as unfettered as U.S. labour markets, he argues, the level of regulation is about the same as in Britain, where labour markets are considerably freer than in continental Europe. Sachs also refers to the WEF survey to argue that Irish labour regulations, unlike those in much of Europe, are not a major hindrance to job creation, and that minimum wage regulations do not set wages so high that they are an important impediment to hiring unskilled or young workers:

> On specific responses to the executive survey carried out by the World Economic Forum, Ireland's minimum wage regulations are *not* deemed to be important barriers to hiring unskilled or young workers, in contrast to the situation in other EU countries. Similarly, Ireland's labour market regulations are *not* seen as seriously impeding the adjustment of labour hours to fluctuations in demand, at least in comparison with other EU countries. In short, Ireland's labour markets are seen as more responsive to market conditions than in other EU countries. (Sachs 1997, 61, italics in the original)

The OECD survey (1997, 88) reviews two studies of the Irish labour market: one finds that Ireland has the third-least-regulated labour market after Switzerland and United Kingdom; the other finds that Ireland has the second-least-regulated labour market after the United Kingdom. However, as discussed elsewhere in this chapter, the combination of Ireland's tax and social-welfare payments may discourage unskilled workers from seeking employment, reducing labour-market flexibility at the lower-wage end of the scale, despite moderate minimum-wage regulations.

A TIME OF GROWTH AND CHANGE

Reduced taxes, fiscal reform, wage moderation, and the promise of higher profits quickly resulted in an increase in investment in both physical and human capital, adding to growth and job creation.

Irish per-capita fixed-capital formation tells the story. Through the 1980s, Ireland's investment position deteriorated significantly. In 1980, Irish capital formation was about 80 per cent of the OECD average, over £1,500 per capita in constant 1990 pounds, by 1986, it was just half the OECD average, a little over £1,100 per capita. Recovery was not instantaneous, but by 1996 capital formation was at its highest level in Irish history. It exceeded 80 per cent of the OECD average and was close to £1,800 per capita – a 60 per cent increase (see charts 2-15 and 2-16).

Yet investment in Ireland has been rather lower than might be expected from the nation's strong economic growth and record of job creation. The ESRI (1997a, 41-42) presents some "plausible reasons" why this might be so. Essentially, the ESRI argues that current investment is more efficient, and thus powers growth even at lower levels than past investment. It also claims that investment has shifted from physical investment to soft investment, which doesn't show up in the numbers. The ESRI argues that, while public-sector investment was high through the 1970s and early 1980s,

> many of the public investment programs were wasteful. In this regard the introduction of long-term planning ... has helped raise the quality of public investment. The restructuring of the manufacturing sector toward more high technology processes has reduced the physical

Chart 2-15 Irish Per Capita Gross Fixed Capital Formation
(OECD = 100)

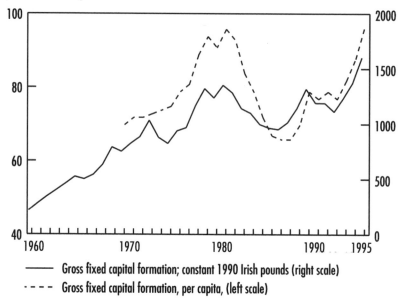

——— Gross fixed capital formation; constant 1990 Irish pounds (right scale)
- - - - Gross fixed capital formation, per capita, (left scale)

Source: OECD National Accounts

Chart 2-16   Irish Per Capita Gross Fixed Capital Formation

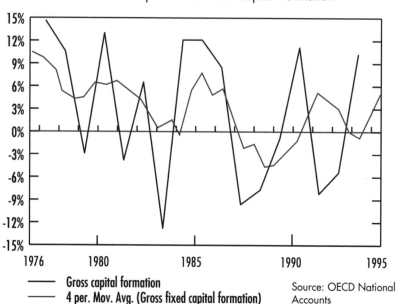

——— Gross capital formation   Source: OECD National
——— 4 per. Mov. Avg. (Gross fixed capital formation)   Accounts

capital-output ratio in production. Most of the investment required in the modern manufacturing sector is quite human-capital and R&D intensive with relatively low plant and capital equipment requirements. (ESRI 1997a, 42)

The reforms also had a profoundly beneficial impact on indigenous business, as Eoin O'Malley reports:

> Since about 1987, there has been a substantial improvement in the growth performance of Irish indigenous industry as measured by trends in employment, output and exports. This improvement has been such that it is without historical precedent in twentieth century Ireland. Not only has the record of Irish indigenous industry been improved by comparison of its own previous experience, but its growth performance over the past decade has also been stronger than that of industrial countries generally. (O'Malley 1998, 57)

According to O'Malley, from 1980 to 1988, permanent employment in indigenous Irish manufacturing industries declined from 143,300 to 110,918, but, by 1997, it had grown to 120,700. Unfortunately, much of O'Malley's data begins in 1985, but the numbers are still telling. Between 1985 and 1987, EU manufacturing output grew at an annual rate of 2.1 per cent, compared to 0.6 per cent for Irish indigenous industry. Between 1987 and 1995, EU output growth had slowed to 1.7 per cent annually; Irish indigenous output was growing at 4.0 per cent a year. O'Malley credits the same factors discussed in this chapter – reduced taxes, wage moderation, deficit control, a better skilled work-force – which benefit all business. He also credits a shift in Irish industrial policy away from subsidies and into helping business improve marketing, management skills, and technology. This removes distortions from the economy, by limiting the "grant-repreneur" mentality while helping firms develop their own expertise.

Econometric work by de la Fuente and Vives (1997) attempts

to quantify the impact of reform on GDP growth. Irish economic growth in the post-1985 period has been about two percentage points (1.95) stronger per year than in the preceding 1970–85 period. De la Fuente and Vives find that improved labour-market performance and fiscal restraint were each responsible for nearly a percentage point in increased annual growth, 0.85 and 0.78 respectively.[10] But, in a sense, this understates the impact of sensible government policies in competing with the rest of the world. Given that bad policy regimes are commonplace, de la Fuente and Vives's work suggests the most important factor in distinguishing Ireland's economic performance from that of other catch-up nations is Ireland's fiscal discipline.

On the labour-market side, one remarkable fact clearly emerges: real wages began to rise rapidly even as unit labour costs were falling. The growth of real wages, under agreements designed to moderate wage growth, differs sharply from the pattern of falling *real* wages during the period unions struggled to achieve the largest wage settlement possible. In the period between 1987, when Irish unions agreed to wage moderation, and 1996, real manufacturing wages rose by 20 per cent and have continued to grow strongly in more recent years. In the period of great union militancy – 1980 to 1984 – real wages fell by six per cent.

Nourishing the Golden Goose

The "golden goose" principle seems to be at work here. When wage increases are moderate and leave a comfortable gap between costs and revenues to maintain profits, strong profits attract further investment, which, in turn, increases the value of labour. This creates room for real wage increases while still leaving strong

---

10. This actually leaves a large part of Ireland's improved performance unexplained by the results. As discussed in other chapters, convergence itself is a strong factor in improving the performance of backward nations. As the Irish economy caught up with advanced economies, convergence weakened as a factor. This should have reduced growth in the post-1985 period by 1.22 percentage points in the model. The other important factor in the model is investment in human capital, which adds 0.40 percentage points to the growth rate.

profits. A virtuous circle is created, benefiting both employer and employee.

However, a vicious circle is also possible. In any given year, labour could bargain for higher wages, which would either substantially reduce or eliminate profits. Either possibility is more attractive for an employer than a lengthy shut-down that would generate negative profits. This inclines employers to accept demands for higher wages, even when these may be damaging in the long run, and it gives unions the power to achieve such increases.

This kills the golden goose. Reduced or disappearing profits remove the incentive for further investment, as well as the resources for investment. Productivity lags. Over time, employers have less and less ability to provide real wage increases. Yet labour will quite naturally expect increases. This can lead to increased labour strife, which further suppresses productivity growth, as the vicious circle turns round. Taken to an extreme, particularly in a fiscally loose climate, which encourages inflation, real wages can begin to fall despite large increases in nominal wages. This is the situation O'Riordan referred to earlier and is indeed the situation Ireland found itself in through the early and mid-1980s.

But, for now, Ireland enjoys a virtuous circle, and the goose continues to lay golden eggs. Moderate wage growth continues to fuel profits, which spur investment, which spurs economic growth and productivity improvements, which allows wages to increase without eating away at profits, and so on. The ability to make profits is Ireland's strongest drawing card for investment (OECD 1997a, 13-19 and see chart 2-17)

Before moving on, two aspects of Ireland's recovery – job creation and Irish GDP growth compared to other advanced nations – bear closer scrutiny.

The Jobless Recovery

Ireland's post-1987 economic recovery was soon dubbed the "jobless recovery". While GDP growth soared, unemployment

Chart 2-17 Rate of Return of US companies
Average 1984-93

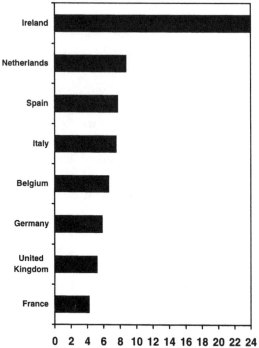

Source: OECD
1997.
Economic
Surveys 1996-
97: Ireland

remained stubbornly high, actually increasing between 1990 and 1993 (see chart 2-18). Part of this is due to long-term unemployment, people who have simply become detached from the labour market and are uninterested in seeking employment. But, in fact, many recoveries are jobless in their initial phases, particularly if the recovery involves a fundamental reordering of the economy.

Increases in productivity ultimately allow companies – and economies – to become more competitive and generate more jobs, but the first step towards efficiency often involves shedding workers. As well, in a rapidly growing, and thus changing, economy, old skills may not be in demand while there may be not enough workers with the necessary skills in the emerging economy. So, in some occupations where workers are plentiful, there are no jobs, and in some occupations, jobs go wanting because there are no

Chart 2-18 Irish Unemployment Rate

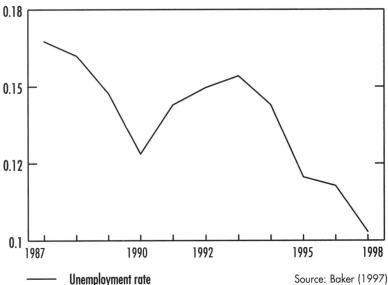

——— **Unemployment rate**   Source: Baker (1997)

workers. In the initial phases of a recovery, these conflicting trends – of new job growth, on one hand, and job shedding and labour-market mismatches, on the other – may roughly balance each other out or even lead to job loss. Only after the economy has gone through this reordering phase does large net job creation usually occur.

This appears to be what happened in Ireland. Job growth was slow in the opening phase of the recovery. From 1987 to 1993, only about 60,000 net new jobs were created, though this is actually a third more net new jobs than were created in the full period from 1971 to 1987.

Job creation took off after 1993. Nearly 200,000 net new jobs were generated from 1993 to 1997. In 1997, for the first time since the early 1970s, the unemployment rate fell into the single digits (below 9 per cent actually). International comparisons highlight the transformation of Ireland's jobs' performance. Between 1981 and 1986, the number of jobs in Ireland fell by 4 per cent. Job growth in the United States was nearly 10 per cent in this period.

In the EU-12, job growth was modest but positive, at 1.6 per cent. But in the decade following 1986, Irish employment growth has been spectacular (26 per cent), far outpacing job growth in the United States (15 per cent) and the EU (7 per cent). Growth in individual years through the mid-1990s tells the story. In 1994, the number of jobs in Ireland grew by 3.1 per cent compared to a *negative* growth rate of 0.3 per cent in the EU; in 1995, Irish job growth was 4.4 per cent compared to positive EU growth of 0.5 per cent; in 1996, Irish job growth was 4.0 per cent compared to 0.1 per cent in the EU; in 1997, Irish job growth was 3.3 per cent compared to 0.4 per cent in the EU (Gray 1997, xxiii).

The reasons for job growth are straightforward:

> Given the combination of good productivity growth and wage restraint, the success of the economy is in a macro sense not hard to explain. With labor relatively inexpensive, the incentives were in place both for high rates of investment and for those investors to choose employment-creating rather than labor-saving techniques of production – a sharp contrast to what was happening in continental Europe. (Krugman 1997, 42-43)

Ironically, one reason for Ireland's spectacular job growth in recent years, and GDP growth, too, was Ireland's bad policy regime through the 1970s and most of the 1980s. This muted the convergence effect through this period, and left the Irish economy further behind advanced economies than it otherwise would have been. Since the magnitude of the convergence effect is related to the size of the gap between advanced and lagging economies, the convergence effect itself helps explain Ireland's rapid economic and employment growth after a sensible policy regime was put in place in the late 1980s.

Ireland Beats the World in GDP Growth
Ireland's GDP growth is particularly impressive when international comparisons are made. From 1981 to 1986, Irish per capita

Chart 2-19 Irish Per Capita GDP

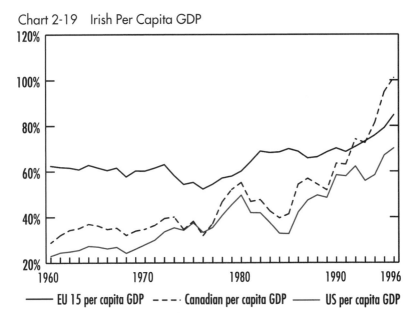

EU 15 per capita GDP ----· Canadian per capita GDP ——— US per capita GDP

Source: OECD Comparative National Accounts

GDP fell substantially in comparison with both Canadian GDP (chart 2-19). Since then, it has risen substantially against both Canadian and U.S. GDP, though this contains a disheartening message about Canada's performance: in the mid-1980s, Canada's per capita GDP was 2.5 times the size of Ireland's; now, Irish per capita GDP exceeds per capita GDP in Canada. Irish per capita GDP has risen to about 70 per cent of U.S. per capita GDP. For most of the 1980s, Irish per capita GDP hovered at about 70 per cent of the EU-15 average, but since 1992 it has risen rapidly to 85 per cent of EU per capita GDP.

One difficulty with Irish GDP measurement is the problem of transfer pricing. One of the ways Ireland pushed costs down for investors was by a dramatic reduction of corporate taxation to 10 per cent in the manufacturing sector. This proved a magnet for investment, but it also created incentives for accounting practices which could distort the true picture of the Irish GDP. Foreign companies had an incentive to attribute as much of their profits as possible to production in Ireland, bloating the GDP accounts. This at first appeared to be a serious problem. In the mid-1990s, economic commentator Jim O'Leary argued that Ireland's economic statistics "had about the same empirical status as moving statues, flying saucers and the statue-of-Elvis-found-on-Mars stories"(Ó Gráda 1997, 33).

This created intense concern in the mid-1990s, with Tansey and others calling for a completely new set of national accounts designed to eliminate the distortion. However, a series of later investigations has revealed that the problem, while it exists, is relatively small. Tansey hardly mentions it in his 1998 book. But this nonetheless points to another problem with Ireland's GDP measure. Because the country has attracted so much foreign investment, there is a considerable outflow of profits each year:

> For most European countries, GDP and GNP are virtually interchangeable. However, in Ireland's case, the scale of annual outflows of factor income – primarily in the form of repatriations of multinational corporate income – have driven a wedge between GDP and GNP. As a result, GDP – broadly, national output – is about 13 per cent higher than national income as measured by GNP. The difference between the two represents the annual amount of income generated by production in Ireland that is transferred abroad. (Tansey 1998, 30; see also the discussion in OECD, 1997a, 18)

It is important to distinguish between the problem of transfer pricing and the GDP–GNP gap. Transfer pricing involves fanciful accounting practices which attribute to Irish-based multinational plants economic activity has actually taken place elsewhere, in order to benefit from Ireland's low rate of corporate tax. This turns out to be a relatively small distortion. The GDP–GNP gap involves economic activity which takes place in Ireland, but the profits of that activity are then exported to other parts of the firm's global structure in returns to shareholders or investments elsewhere.

A sizeable portion of Ireland's output in this way is transferred as profits into foreign hands. It is worth noting that I have not found a single article, book, or publication in Ireland that criticizes this flow, nor did I talk to one person in Ireland who mentioned it as a problem. The view seems to be that the output wouldn't be there in the first place were it not for foreign investment. This was the route to growth taken by the United States through most of its history, particularly when it was a developing economy.

OTHER FACTORS

A number of other factors contributed to Ireland's economic growth since 1987. Most important in the long run is an improved education and training system. In the shorter term, a devaluation of the Irish pound in 1986 was, as discussed earlier, a key factor in the almost painless transition to fiscal responsibility. A further devaluation of the pound in 1993, coming on the heels of Ireland's participation in the European single-market project in 1992, doubtless helped Irish growth in the latter part of the 1990s, though many believe this devaluation presents a problem. Ireland's strong productivity growth hardly justified devaluation, which threatened to overheat the economy and lead to inflation. Fortunately for Ireland, wage agreements held, and inflation remained under control.

An Educated and Growing Work-force

The Irish education story is particularly important, though it is too far outside the range of this book, which focuses on macro-economic policies, to discuss it at length. Ireland was late in granting free secondary education to youths. This occurred only in 1968 and helped lay the groundwork for recent growth, although not until other macro-policies were in place. The first cadre benefiting from free secondary education entered the work-force in the early to mid-1970s, but many of them, particularly those with post-secondary education, emigrated because of poor economic conditions in Ireland. Nonetheless, by the time of the policy turnabout of the late 1980s, Ireland's populace had broader and better education than ever before in the nation's history. The availability of educated workers for the jobs being created, particularly in the high-tech sector, sustained and furthered Ireland's recovery.

Ireland also advanced its technological, technical, and trades training programmes and institutions, as well as establishing new apprenticeship programmes. As can be seen from chart 2-17, the availability of skilled workers and the educational level of the workforce are both powerful attractions for investment. In Europe, only Germany scores higher for availability of skilled workers, and Ireland leads the pack on relevance of education.

Many Irish commentators believe the increasingly well-educated and well-trained Irish work-force will continue to propel growth, particularly as younger workers enter the work-force and older, less-skilled workers retire. This also highlights Ireland's favourable demographics. Through the 1990s, the labour force should increase by about 2 per cent a year, though Ireland's slowing birth rate will reduce labour-force growth in future years.

The current increase in the work-force – rather than creating a drag on the economy, as it sometimes has in the past, when the labour force grew more rapidly than employment – should help sustain Ireland's growth as the demand for skilled labour increases. Although shortages of skilled workers are already apparent, the growth of the labour force will mitigate the negative effects. Reforms of the social-welfare system, designed to make work a more attractive alternative to social-welfare payments at the bottom end of the income scale will also boost labour-force growth. This, too, is positive, since shortages of low-skilled workers have begun to appear, though they are not as acute as shortages for high-skilled workers. As well, training programmes have been targeted to help these workers to increase their skills.

The situation is summed up in the ESRI's *Medium-Term Review: 1997-2003* (1997a):

Over the last decade the Irish labour market has been

profoundly affected by a number of different factors which have altered the supply of labour. These factors include changing demographic trends, rising female participation rates and the medium and long-term effects of changes in domestic policies in the education system and the social welfare system. These policy changes have had the effect of increasing the supply of skilled labour and gradually reducing the supply of unskilled labour. This has led to an increase in the stock of human capital and the rate of human capital accumulation. (47; for a more extensive discussion, see pages 7–33 in the same publication)

European Union Funds

Two other factors are often cited for Ireland's recent success, though they have played a relatively small role. These factors are EU subsidies to Ireland and Ireland's business subsidies. Canadian commentators, in particular, tend to focus on these elements of Irish recovery, perhaps to justify similar policies in Atlantic Canada.

EU subsidies have clearly helped Ireland, but both the size of the transfers and their use distinguish them from the Atlantic Canadian experience. Total transfers rose from just over 5 per cent of GDP in 1986 to a peak of 7 per cent in 1991, and have now fallen to about 4 per cent of GDP. This compares to net transfers to Atlantic Canada which peaked at about 40 per cent of GDP and are now equal to between a quarter and a fifth of GDP (see *Retreat from Growth* (McMahon 2000)). The actual per-capita transfers are even more unbalanced, since, through much of this period, Atlantic Canada's per capita GDP exceeded Ireland's. If such transfers were a significant part of the story, Atlantic Canada should have raced ahead of Ireland instead of falling well behind.

EU transfers need to be broken into two key component parts, each of roughly equal weight. One component is EU agricultural subsidies. These boost rural incomes but have little impact on investment and may retard economic adjustment by keeping rural populations artificially high. Yet, despite these subsidies, Ireland's rural population and income continue to shrink. (See *Retreat from Growth* (McMahon 2000) for a fuller discussion of rural development.)

EU structural funds are the other key component. These are meant to build economically important infrastructure. Unlike in Atlantic Canada, where transfers seem to have added little to useful economic infrastructure – aside from failing coal mines, heavy-water plants, a money-losing steel mill, and a proliferation of fish plants and fishing vessels chasing often-declining stocks – Irish policy-makers, particularly the ESRI and the NESC, carefully track the use of EU transfers to ensure they are directed to useful investment, though some fungibility is probably inevitable. Nonetheless, Irish policy-makers set high standards for the use of EU structural funds. As the ESRI says in its 1997 evaluation of EU structural fund expenditures:

> Our evaluation ... begins with the premise that the opportunity cost of public funds is high. All public spending must be measured on a competitive basis against the best alternative use of funds. It is not enough to say that a particular expenditure is within budget and contributing to the goals set for it. We must try to assess whether it could be better spent. (ESRI 1997b, xv)

Economic Development Subsidies

Ireland's use of industrial incentives through the Industrial Development Agency (IDA) Ireland to attract investment has also generated much attention in Atlantic Canada, but considerably less attention in Ireland. The IDA's performance never came up in the interviews I conducted in Ireland unless I introduced the topic. In the several thousand pages on the Irish experience I have reviewed, the IDA is seldom mentioned, and, when it is, the discussion often concerns some controversial aspect of its performance (Ó Gráda 1997, 54; 113-128).

In fact, subsidies were reduced as part of Ireland's fiscal reforms in 1987, yet the loss of subsidies certainly did not slow the powerful growth, the strongest in Ireland's history, that followed these reforms. The IDA's subsidy muscle was strongest in the early 1980s, yet growth was slow despite IDA intervention. By the early 1990s, IDA subsidies were at about half the level of a decade earlier, yet growth was strong.

In the OECD (1997a) report on Ireland, the IDA is mentioned only once and then only as the source of information for a chart. The IDA is not listed in the index of any of the books I've reviewed on Ireland.[11] Interestingly, IDA officials themselves do not credit the subsidy game as being a particularly important part of the Irish economic story, save in one regard – as a defensive strategy against other jurisdictions which offer large subsidies. In fact, the IDA is highly critical of the subsidy game:

> [T]he trends in continental Europe – and especially in more centrally located areas – for increased financial incentives to secure foreign investment is of concern to us, both from a cost-efficiency point of view and its logic. (Irish Development Agency 1995)

IDA officials rightly take pride in their marketing abilities – bringing to the attention of foreign firms the strengths of Ireland as a profitable place for investment. Here, their marketing arsenal is full and effective. It focuses on costs in the economy – the tax structure, in particular the 10 per cent corporate tax rate,[12] and labour costs. It is worth noting that these low cost factors are simply part of the economic landscape and thus avoid the pathologies

11. Though this may be somewhat deceptive. The IDA is mentioned briefly in both Ó Gráda and Gray, and more extensively in O'Sullivan (1995), though it is not found in the index to these books. Nonetheless, Irish analysts simply do not consider the IDA a key part of the Irish economic story in the way Atlantic Canadians once fastened their hopes on various subsidy agencies to attract investment.

12. This, and much of the Irish tax structure, is under review. In particular, the EU has been clear in its displeasure with Ireland's tax competition, which is seen on the continent as a key reason for Ireland's economic success.

of politically motivated subsidies discussed in the next volume. In its marketing, the IDA ties the cost advantages of Ireland to its open economy and the attractiveness of the European market. According to IDA officials, subsidies do not attract companies to Ireland; they are merely a defensive measure against subsidies granted elsewhere.

As O'Sullivan notes, Ireland's industrial incentive policy has been in place since the early 1950s, but rapid economic growth only followed the macro-economic reforms. During Ireland's weakest period of growth, 1981 to 1986, Ireland's industrial aid, as a percentage of manufacturing gross value added, reached 12.3 per cent, more than twice the European average, but obviously these aids were ineffective in spurring economy-wide growth. They declined to 6.4 per cent in the period 1986 to 1988, compared to a European average of 4 per cent. They were lowest as Ireland's growth took off between 1988 and 1990, at 4.9 per cent, compared to a European average of 3.5 per cent (O'Sullivan 1995, 383; she does not present numbers for the years after 1992).

De la Fuente and Vives (1997, 104–5) provide a GDP-based calculation of subsidies which also shows a roll-back. From 1980 to 1984, subsidies equalled 3.5 per cent of GDP; from 1990 to 1994, a period of strong growth, subsidies equalled 1.1 per cent of GDP. As de la Fuente and Vives show, the subsidy cut-backs were not motivated by improved economic times but by Ireland's aggressive moves to cut back government in order to lower taxes, which in turn generated new growth.

In any event, it is difficult to credit subsidies, at their lowest level, with Ireland's strong growth in recent years, when one considers the much higher subsidies in the 1980s during Ireland's experiment with a large interventionist government, a period of dismal growth and job creation. The clear consensus among Irish economists is that fundamental economic reforms – wage moderation, tax cuts, reductions in the size of government, etc. – spurred the recent growth, not industrial incentives.

KILLING THE GOLDEN GOOSE

Good times are already beginning to chase away the memories of bad times – and the memories of why tough medicine was needed to cure Ireland's economic malaise. Although the union leadership remains committed to wage moderation, the membership has become restive. Large minorities of union membership now vote against wage-moderation agreements, and inflationary fires have begun to burn under the Irish economy.

Government policies are part of the problem. After large reductions in government expenditure as a percentage of GDP between 1986 and 1989, expenditures have begun to creep up again. Tansey, one of the key architects of the 1987–88 turn-around, is highly critical of the government's action (Tansey 1998, particularly pp. 175-240). Real growth in spending has been exceeding even the red-hot growth of the economy, and so the expenditure-to-GDP ratio has steadily edged upward since 1989. Although this ratio remains substantially below the levels through the first seven years of the 1980s, government is clearly expanding its role in the economy again.

Increasing spending could not come at a more difficult time. If anything, Irish growth has been too strong, threatening an overheating. To the extent that the old Keynesian mechanisms work at all, the prescription would be restrained government spending. The fiscal side of the equation becomes even more important now that Ireland does not have monetary mechanisms to dampen economic activity. That, of course, is because of European monetary union in which Ireland is an enthusiastic participant. But growth on the continent is sluggish. Thus, the continental interest rates which European monetary union will bring to Ireland are far lower than are suitable for Ireland's red-hot economy.

The other side of government, taxation, has steadily moved up as well. Although a number of agreements have limited taxes, the tax take again has risen even faster than growth, perhaps because, as the Irish become richer, more of the GDP is taxed at higher marginal rates. Ireland's newest labour pact contains the promise of further tax cuts, so how all this will balance out in the long run remains an open question.

The number of jobs in Ireland has soared, and the unemployment rate has fallen dramatically even though the labour force is growing dramatically. From 1994 to 1997, over 50,000 additional jobs were created each year. In 1998, the number of jobs in Ireland rose by nearly 100,000. Unemployment has fallen each year, and by mid-1999, it dropped below 6 per cent.

This is partially revealed by the gap between Live Registered Unemployment and the Labour Force Survey, as discussed earlier. Doubtless even the survey overstates real unemployment, as some who are not truly seeking work will claim to be. Shortages are already showing up in the labour market, putting further pressure on wages. While the unions try to police wage settlements, some employers are making under-the-table payments to employees to maintain their services. While labour shortages are most extreme in high-skill jobs, like computer programmers, shortages of many different types of workers are common, as reflected in an article from the *Irish Independent* (20 June 1998, 6):

> Top chefs such as Michael Martin at Dublin's Clarence Hotel constantly receive job offers. Michael Martin estimates he receives 10 job offers a year ... "We like to play by the rule book here, but there is a lot of poaching of staff now in Dublin. I know of places where they are offering under the table payments of £600" [Martin is quoted as saying].

The same article notes that bricklayers can earn over £250 a day, or over $100,000 Canadian over the course of a year. The headline "Skilled workers who can't afford a job" reflects the fact that the labour market is so tight that skilled workers can often earn more freelancing than in full-time work where wage scales are covered by Ireland's labour pacts.

Sachs (1997, 63) notes the "risk to Ireland's export-led growth model. Ireland must maintain cost competitiveness, with changes in wage levels appropriately reflecting changes in productivity and world-wide demand for Ireland's products." The wage agreements discussed earlier are typically in part based on research on such things as productivity growth. But if such agreements come un-ravelled, Ireland is in a more precarious position than in the past. Previously, for example, in 1986 and 1993, Ireland was able to use devaluation when domestic costs reached uncompetitive lev-els. With the move toward a single European currency, this will not be possible in the future.

So, as suggested in the first chapter, the corporatist turn-around may be time-limited. The key costs Ireland struggled to reduce in the late 1980s may soon start growing again. Despite strong eco-nomic growth, taxes have increased as a percentage of GDP; un-controlled economic growth could lead to another bout of infla-tion and its associated costs; and the labour agreements are in danger of coming unravelled.

Yet, whether or not the Irish economy continues to grow at its present pace or becomes derailed, it has pointed to key aspects of policy which can lead to accelerated economic and employment growth. The question is whether these will be maintained in fu-ture years.

CONCLUSION

For generations, Ireland had been the most economically back-ward nation in northern Europe. Unable to generate enough pros-perity and jobs for even its small population, Ireland exported people rather than goods and services. Independence did little to change this dismal situation − Ireland still lagged behind all its neighbours, and economic refugees continued to flee the island.

Ireland's experiment with a closed economy and job genera-tion through import substitution was an unmitigated disaster. It isolated Ireland from the powerful wave of growth and prosperity that swept through western Europe after the end of World War II. The results were so dismal that even the architects of the closed-door policy reversed course to open the Irish economy to world competition at the end of the 1950s.

Thus began Ireland's first golden economic age. Ireland generated jobs and wealth faster than it ever had in its history. But this was short-lived. Growing public expenditure, an increasing tax burden, mounting government intervention in the economy, rising debts and deficits, and union militancy pushed up costs in the Irish economy. Profits virtually disappeared and so did investment. Unemployment rose and "the culture of employment" was lost to a whole sector of Irish society, people who joined the rolls of the long-term unemployed. As bad as things had been in the past, this proved to be the most dismal economic period in twentieth-century Irish economic history, for the earlier glimpse of prosperity had turned to ashes.

Bad times concentrated policy thinking. Irish society as a whole reached a consensus in the late 1980s that costs had to be reduced in the economy. Unions adopted wage moderation as their creed. Government slashed expenditures and taxes. Profits rose rapidly, creating a magnet for further investment.

The results were remarkable. They didn't simply better Ireland's own dismal economic history; Ireland's record of GDP growth is now the strongest in the developed world. In the early and mid-1980s, Irish unemployment had climbed to nearly 20 per cent. Now Ireland faces a labour shortage.

Tax cuts and wage moderation, far from reducing tax revenues and real wages, led to dramatic increases. Revenues are higher now than when tax rates were at their peak. The Irish have gone from being one of the most poorly paid people in the developed world to one of the best paid. What many feared would be a "race to the bottom" became a rapid climb to new economic heights.

Chapter 3
The Dutch Miracle

[W]e have been swamped in recent months by requests
from foreign visitors/journalists who want to know
about the "Dutch Polder Model". A sense of euphoria
is growing among politicians and the trade unions, no
doubt partly as a result of foreign admiration.
— *VNO-NCW (1997b)*

INTRODUCTION AND OVERVIEW

Much Dutch commentary on the nation's strong economic performance contains something like a sense of wonder – just 15
years ago the economy was one of the worst performing in western Europe and now it is the star of the continental class. The
story is similar to Ireland's. Government cut its expenditures and
reduced taxes. Unions, business, and government signed a series
of wage-moderation pacts explicitly targeted at increasing profits
in the Dutch economy. One additional ingredient is found in the
Netherlands's success. Unlike Ireland, the Netherlands had established a heavy overhang of regulations, increasing costs in the
economy. Government has launched a deregulation effort and
begun a privatization programme.

The Netherlands has been so successful that a touch of exas-
peration may accompany comments about the horde of policy-
makers, politicians, journalists, and economists descending on the
Netherlands in an attempt to learn the secret of what is variously
called the Tulip Miracle, the Dutch Model, or, often, the Polder
Model.[1] These commentaries then almost inevitably point out that
there is no such model, just a series of realistic consensual

---

1. *Polder* simply means land claimed from the sea through dikes.

decisions sparked by the disastrous shape of the Dutch economy in the early 1980s and a repeat performance of economic troubles in the early 1990s. This is correct. While the Netherlands's recent economic growth and, most particularly, employment generation have resulted from a significant ongoing policy shift, on a deeper level the Dutch success is not a model in itself. It is rather a set of policy alternatives within the larger corporatist model or structure. And the Dutch experience shows the strengths and weaknesses of this model. The evolution of the Dutch economy highlights what may be the time-limited nature of successful growth policies in a corporatist setting.

The Dutch have been through what might be thought of as the corporatist cycle. In the immediate aftermath of World War II, a society-wide consensus – one involving labour, business, and government – held down costs, particularly wage costs, throughout the economy. Dutch economic growth was strong and unemployment vanishingly low in the post-war period. Although this consensus began to unravel in the 1960s, Dutch economic growth remained strong into the 1970s, in part boosted by a large natural-gas find that topped up both the economy and government coffers.

But, as we shall see, this natural-resource wealth turned out to be a curse in disguise. "On the one hand, this discovery reduced [the Netherlands's] energy import dependency. On the other hand, it contributed to the unsustainable expansion of the welfare state, which set the stage for a serious crisis at the end of the seventies and early eighties" (CPB 1997, 14). It is worth noting that the CPB – the Central Planning Bureau – is a joint labour/business/government body, and this statement reflects a broad consensus in the Netherlands.

These developments laid the groundwork for the disaster about to befall the Dutch economy in the 1970s. As the Dutch consensus on wages restraint fell apart, wages soared through the 1970s and into the 1980s. As wage costs got out of hand, unemployment – which had not been a serious problem to this point in the post-war period – skyrocketed to over 17 per cent in 1984. Between 1981 and 1983, nearly 300,000 jobs were lost. In 1984, 10,000 people were added to the unemployment rolls each month, until the number reached 800,000. Economic growth hovered close to zero through much of the 1980s.

Government played a perverse role in these unfolding events. Encouraged in part by the flow of natural-gas revenues, government expenditures grew spectacularly through the 1970s and early 1980s, from 40 per cent of GDP in 1973 to 58 per cent in 1983. This crowded out private-sector activity. Generous government social-assistance programmes provided the foundation for the escalation in wages. People could choose not to work and accept social assistance if wages did not meet their expectations. This pushed up the reservation wage – that is the wage workers require before they will accept a job. And, despite natural-gas revenues, the government's fiscal position rapidly deteriorated.

As in Ireland, nothing concentrates the mind better than economic disaster. In 1982, the Netherlands took the first step down the road to controlling costs and economic recovery. Much to everyone's surprise, labour and business signed an agreement designed to restrain wages. Market forces had already begun to put downward pressure on wages. Wage growth continued to cool until the late 1980s. Through the same period, government began to rein in expenditures. With the exception of a blip upward in 1987, government expenditures as a percentage of GDP glided downward until about 1990, and then began to creep upwards again.

In the late 1980s and early 1990s, the corporatist consensus was once again unravelling. Not only was government expenditure on the rise, but danger signs began to warn about problems with labour costs. Dutch unit labour costs moved up from 1985 to 1992 almost as sharply as they had from the early 1970s to 1980. Job growth came to a halt in the early 1990s, and the unemployment rate once again began to grow. Dutch per capita GDP started to dip relative to U.S. and OECD per capita GDP. The early 1990s began to look like the early 1980s, with rising costs suppressing economic growth and job creation.

But the lessons of the 1980s were still fresh. A new labour compact negotiated in 1993 and implemented in 1994 stabilized Dutch unit labour costs. In fact, unit labour costs sharply declined in 1993 and 1994. Employment growth, which had fallen to zero in 1993, recovered. Dutch per capita GDP began to grow strongly again. A new left–right (purple) coalition, led by a former labour leader, began a serious attack on government spending, pushing it down toward 50 per cent of GDP.

Dutch monetary policy through most of the period after World War II tended to be passive. In times of inflation, monetary growth typically accommodated increased government expenditures and rising wage demands. Nor did the authorities typically attempt to spur economic activity through monetary expansion. Through the Netherlands's weakest economic period in the 1970s and early 1980s, already high levels of inflation ruled out this course of action.

The Corporatist Cycle

The Dutch have been through the corporatist cycle several times – consensus on controlling costs, particularly wage moderation, in the immediate post-war period, leading to strong economic growth; bickering in the 1960s, followed by out-of-control costs and economic decline in the 1970s; a weak social agreement on wage moderation in the early 1980s, which led to increased economic growth in much of the 1980s; a near breakdown of the social consensus on wages in the early 1990s, threatening the Dutch economic revival; and, more recently, a much stronger agreement on wage moderation and tax reduction. This led to period often termed the "Dutch miracle", characterized by strong economic growth and job creation. "Like the economy, the Dutch consultation process has gone through various upward and downward trends throughout its development" (van Empel 1997, 13).

Another factor separates the Irish corporatist experiment from the Dutch. Ireland took extremely strong measures across the board in restraining taxes and wages in 1987. Ireland's economic take-off was also extremely powerful. The first round of the Dutch cure in 1982 was much less radical for both wages and government taxes/expenditure. As a result, the cure was considerably less robust. The Dutch took a much more vigorous course of treatment in 1993-94, with a stronger commitment to hold down wage costs, reduce government expenditures, reform and privatize social programs, and vitalize market forces. The result was also more vigorous. It led to the strong economic growth and job creation known today as the "Dutch miracle".

Another difference is that the Irish seem to believe their work is almost done, save for some revamping of the tax code and income-support system to make work more rewarding and social assistance less appealing. The Dutch still have an ambitious agenda of market reforms and government-expenditure cuts before them.

The reason is partly because the Dutch reforms on the government side remain less deep than Irish reforms. Dutch government expenditures are higher as a percentage of GDP than Irish expenditures. However, Dutch expenditures continue to decline relative to GDP, while Irish expenditures are now rising. And the Dutch have a heavy regulatory build-up to tackle, while the Irish economy has never been overly regulated. The questions for the future in the Netherlands are: Will these corporatist reform plans wither with the good times when reform simply seems unnecessary? Will the corporatist cycle continue to turn?

BIRTH OF THE CORPORATIST MODEL

Consensual decision-making has long been part of the Dutch character, going back several centuries to the development of the Dutch merchant society. The foundation for the current corporatist state was laid in the 1920s, if not earlier. Nearly 40 per cent of all employees were members of a trade union by 1920. Unions became increasingly involved in decision-making – including wage negotiations – at the national and sectoral levels. However, unions had less influence at the level of the firm, due to employer opposition.

At the national level, the *Hooge Raad van Arbeid* (Supreme Labour Council) was established in the 1920s as a consultative council involving labour, employers, and government. In 1927, the collective-agreement act was passed, giving stronger legal status to collective agreements. In 1937, a new act allowed government to extend collective agreements in one sector to all employees of that sector, regardless of whether workers or their companies had participated in the negotiations. These developments formed the basis for the post-war experience.

The construction of the Dutch corporatist state was completed in the early post-war period. The Netherlands had been slow to industrialize in the pre-war period, and much of its industrial base and infrastructure had been destroyed in the war. Dutch policy-makers, faced with a small home market, decided on a course of rapid industrialization and export growth. The engine for this growth would be a low-cost economy. "It was therefore necessary to restrain wages and produce more cheaply than in neighbouring countries. In the first decade after the war there was a near complete consensus about this strategy ..." (Visser & Hemerijck 1997, 92).

In May 1945, employers and employees established the Labour Foundation (STAR)[2] as a consultative forum for the two groups. It was meant to aid in sharing of information and ideas, and to help create a bond between employers and employees. It remains a key anchor of the corporatist state. The Labour Foundation, in partnership with the government, negotiated wage guidelines, which were formally issued by the Board of Government Mediators (CvR).

In 1950, the Labour Foundation was supplemented by the formation of the Social and Economic Council (SER), which included employers, employees, and economic experts appointed by the government. These structures effectively and almost without opposition set wages and maintained wage moderation from 1945 until the 1960s, a period of strong growth and effectively zero unemployment. The strength of these arrangements can be seen

---

2. Acronyms are, of course, of Dutch words and will not usually match the English translation.

Chart 3-1 Real Hourly Compensation in Dutch Manufacturing
(1992 = 100)

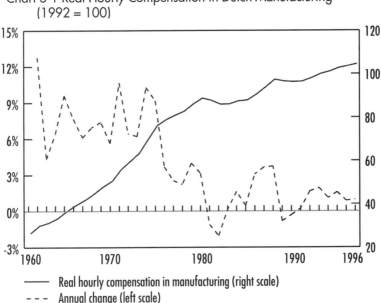

Real hourly compensation in manufacturing (right scale)
- - - Annual change (left scale)

Source: U.S. Bureau of Labor Statistics

in a 1951 agreement under which labour, business, and government jointly agreed that nominal wages should be pushed down
by 5 per cent.

The Netherlands was a low-cost economy. This led to a remarkable burst of economic growth and job creation. That held
the seeds to the unravelling of the social agreement. The economy
overheated, and that, combined with low-cost wages, led to labour shortages. The labour shortage was such that employers began to use "black wages" – under-the-table payments above and
beyond the wages levels established by the CvR – to attract workers. The necessity of maintaining a low-cost economy seemed to
evaporate. Wages exploded. Real-wage increases averaged about
8 per cent a year (chart 3-1). Unions simply could not tell members to accept CvR guidelines when employers were willing to
pay more.

During the first long, steady economic upswing after the Second World War, the consultation model was at least as successful as it is today. Indeed, so great was this success [in holding down costs to boost economic growth] that it almost spelled the end of the consultation model. Wages were so restrained, and the competitive powers of Dutch trade and industry grew so dramatically that tension began to rise in the labour market.... The summer of 1962 saw the start of a long period of large wage hikes and labour unrest which would only come to an end in the early eighties. (van Empel 1997, 13-14)

Acrimony became common in industrial relations. The major Catholic and Protestant labour federations, later united in the FNV, temporarily withdrew from both STAR and SER in 1970, in protest against a wage act that attempted to restore wage moderation. Although industrial unrest remained lower in the Netherlands than in most European nations, the number of strikes grew, and a split emerged between moderate union leadership and a new generation of more radical leaders. Both wages and the Dutch unemployment rate crept up through the 1970s. Unemployment exploded late in the decade, peaking at 17 per cent in 1984 (chart 3-2).

Increasing government expenditure played a role in the Netherlands's emerging economic problems, particularly under the centre–left government of Joop den Uyl (1974-77), though, as with Ireland, the process really got under way with the first oil crisis.

A number of countries, including the Netherlands, reacted by Keynesian demand policy, but they found that this medicine did not have substantial influence any more on economic growth and employment. At the same time, government expenditures increased and inflation took off. Economic policy seemed to have lost control. (CPB 1997, 81)

Government, itself, even before transfer payments, was consuming an ever greater portion of GDP (chart 3-3).

Chart 3-2 Dutch Unemployment Rate

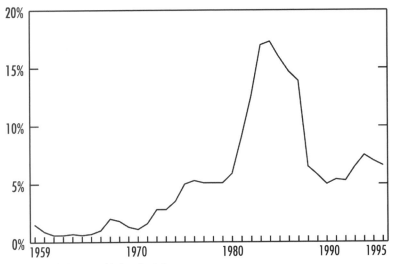

Source: U.S. Bureau of Labor Statistics

The 1970s were the era of "Dutch disease", when government expenditures, fuelled by large natural-gas revenues, took off.

> The Dutch government introduced an expansionary policy, financed by the abundant revenues from natural gas. The 1970s are the era of the Dutch Disease, characterized by inflation, expanding government expenditures and sharply declining profits. (Nickell & van Ours 1999, 18)

A key area of expenditure was the development of rich social programmes, which created an incentive for Dutch workers to leave the work-force to collect benefits, something we'll look at in more depth later in this chapter. This development added to the wage pressure created by the breakdown in consensual bargaining. The Netherlands was becoming an increasingly expensive place to do business.

Expenditures had soared under the den Uyl government, and they continued to rise under succeeding governments, including the badly divided centre–right coalition of Andries van Agt (1977–

Chart 3-3   Dutch Government Consumption

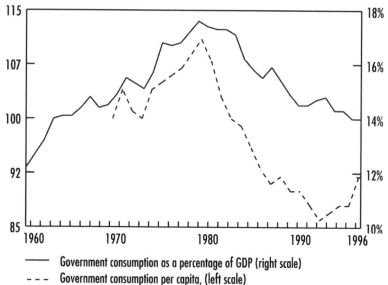

—— Government consumption as a percentage of GDP (right scale)
- - - Government consumption per capita, (left scale)

Source: OECD National Accounts

81) and the unstable centre–left coalition, also under van Agt, which followed. By early 1982, government expenditures equalled more than 55 per cent of GDP. Rising taxes fuelled the wage explosion, as workers attempted to make up in higher pay their increasing losses to government.

Unfortunately, much of this spending only went to distort further the labour market and to add to wage inflation. The government established a number of social programmes which enabled Dutch workers to leave the labour market or refuse to join it unless employers bid well above the level of social assistance available through a number of different programmes, particularly the nation-wide disability scheme. Such systems take on a life of their own. Over the years, they attract more and more people into the social net and discourage people from leaving. This pushes up expenditures years after the measures were passed.

By the mid-1980s, social-security payments alone reached 20 per cent of GDP. At the same time, for every five people employed, four people were collecting some form of benefit. If one

Chart 3-4   Inactive/active Ratios & Social Security Outlays

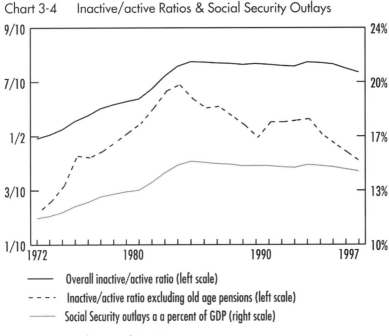

Overall inactive/active ratio (left scale)

- - - - Inactive/active ratio excluding old age pensions (left scale)

Social Security outlays a a percent of GDP (right scale)

Source: Visser and Hemerijck (1997)

excludes old-age-pension payments, which often went to relatively young people who had retired early, the ratio was still above two people on benefits for every five employed. Chart 3-4 plots these inactive/active ratios. It also shows social-security outlays. These outlays as a percentage of GDP begin to decline prior to declines in the inactive/active ratio. This is because of reductions in real terms in benefits.

Nonetheless, the social-security system still provided relatively high levels of benefits and continued to draw people out of the work-force. High taxes made wage work even less desirable. All this also meant the official unemployment rate greatly understated the combined rate of involuntary and voluntary unemployment. And it pulled less-skilled workers out of the job market into long-term unemployment, meaning skills would further erode and those involved in this trap would become less and less employable. A key part of the problem was a wrong wage differentiation, brought about by a policy of leveling incomes. The statutory minimum wage and minimum social benefits were substantially raised in respect to the average wage level. The victims were the low-skilled workers. Existing jobs became too costly and were scrapped. New ones were blocked. (Klaver 1997, 3)

These factors drastically cut the number of low-skill, entry-level jobs in the Netherlands. At the same time, generous social assistance discouraged low-skill workers from taking what employment was available. This led in the Netherlands, as it did in Ireland, to the creation of a pool of long-term unemployed. Even today, as job growth soars in the Netherlands, half the unemployed have been without work for a year, and fully four-fifths for more than six months. This compares with 10 and 17 per cent of the unemployed in the United States,[3] even though job growth has been greater in the Netherlands than in the United States in recent years. And these unemployment figures, as we shall see, don't include huge numbers of Dutch on various disability and income-support schemes.

A high-cost economy had replaced a low-cost economy. By the mid-1970s, the textile, clothing, and shipbuilding industries were all in trouble, despite large government subsidies meant to rescue them. Wage costs were soaring out of control, and unit labour costs were rising rapidly compared to those of the Netherlands's competitors (charts 3-5, 3-6 and 3-7). Inflation and its assorted costs were on the rise (chart 3-8). Taxes were increasing, and the ballooning debt and deficit promised even more taxes down the road. Just as forward-looking expectations can help an economy grow when tax reduction is on the horizon, it can damage GDP growth when tax increases are expected. All these factors contributed to weaken GDP growth. Dutch GDP fell relative to that of most other advanced economies. It would not rise again until measures were put back in place to control costs in the economy (charts 3-9 and 3-10).

---

3. These numbers can be found in Netherlands (1997, 190).

Chart 3-5   Dutch Unit Labour Costs (1992 = 100)

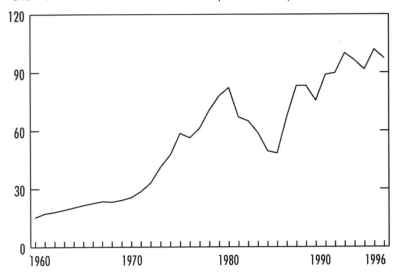

Source: U.S. Bureau of Labor Statistics

Chart 3-6   Evolution of Dutch Unit Labour Costs

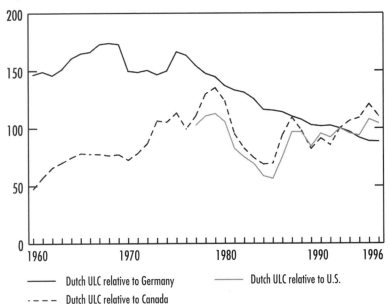

——— Dutch ULC relative to Germany   ——— Dutch ULC relative to U.S.
- - - - Dutch ULC relative to Canada

Source: U.S. Bureau of Labor Statistics

Chart 3-7   Evolution of Hourly Manufacturing Wages
(1992 = 100; based on U.S. exchange rate)

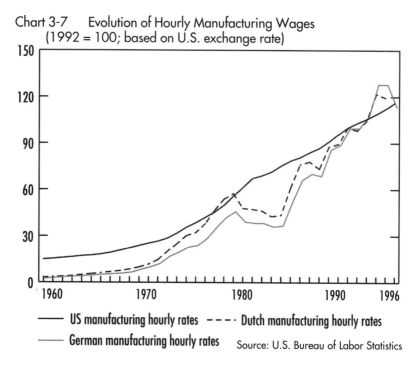

——— US manufacturing hourly rates   - - - - Dutch manufacturing hourly rates
——— German manufacturing hourly rates   Source: U.S. Bureau of Labor Statistics

Chart 3-8   Dutch Consumer Price Index (1990 = 100)

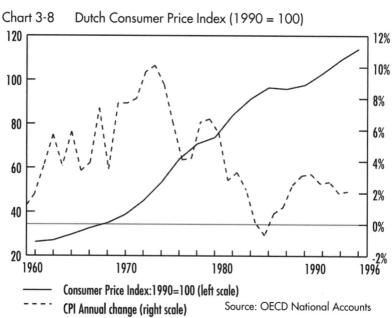

——— Consumer Price Index:1990=100 (left scale)
- - - - CPI Annual change (right scale)   Source: OECD National Accounts

Chart 3-9 Dutch Real GDP (1990 = 100)

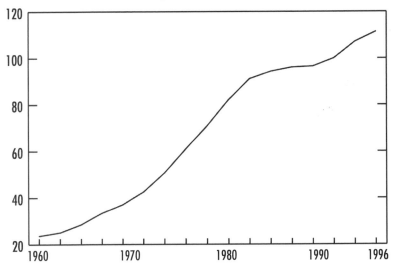

Source: OECD National Accounts

Chart 3-10   Dutch Per Capita GDP (OECD = 100)

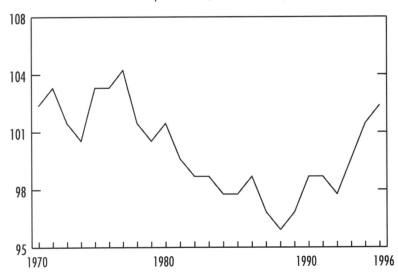

Source: OECD National Accounts

This high-cost, big-government economy, characterized by union militancy, was "Dutch disease" at its most virulent. Given the Dutch history of economic success, the negative consequences were dramatic. Not only did unemployment rise, but hundreds of thousands of jobs were destroyed. Dutch per capita GDP declined relative to that of other advanced nations. Dutch policy-makers began to understand the negative consequences of a high-cost economy, even for those it was supposed to benefit, well-paid union members. Not only were jobs disappearing, but real wages were stagnant or declining. The next two decades would be spent trying to reverse Dutch disease. When wage moderation was restored to the economy and tax cuts introduced, prosperity and job creation were quickly restored to the Dutch economy.

WASSENAAR

The Dutch economy was particularly hard hit by the energy crisis of 1979. This was in part because generous social-assistance schemes kept wages high and limited the economy's ability to adjust to reduced demand in Europe, which was also reeling from the oil crisis. The Netherlands's petrochemical wealth was a curse despite high energy prices. It enabled the Dutch to continue funding perverse programmes. Unemployment rose, GDP growth was often negative, and the deficit rose despite natural-gas revenues. The Dutch economy seemed set for a long-term downward spiral. This bout of Dutch disease was a big contrast with what was to come. "Whereas the term 'Dutch disease' was coined 20 years ago for the practice of using natural gas sales to build a generous social security system, nowadays, the 'Dutch Model' is held up as an example for other continental European economies" (VNO-NCW 1997a, 45).

Bad times can lead to desperate measures, including the willingness to compromise for the greater good and to make hard decisions. A number of attempts to re-establish nationwide wage guidelines had failed. But then, to virtually everyone's surprise, the Wassenaar pact emerged in 1982. Chris van Veen was head of the Dutch employers' organization (the Confederation of Netherlands Industry and Employers, VNO-NCW). He shared child-rearing responsibilities with his working wife and frequently had to stay at home. Thus it was that he often held meetings at his home in Wassenaar, outside The Hague, with his labour counter-part – someone who will emerge later in another, even more im-portant role – Wim Kok, head of the Dutch Trades Unions, the FNV, the largest federation of unions in the Netherlands. The Wassenaar agreement was pounded out on van Veen's kitchen table.

The agreement focused on wage moderation and on improv-ing private sector profits. Profits had fallen to a level that sup-pressed the funds available for investment and virtually eliminated the incentive to invest. The income share of capital fell from 19 per cent in 1970 to 7 per cent in 1983. (In 1998, the capital income share is expected to be 21 per cent.) (Klaver 1997). The SER's outlook paper, *Socio-economic policy 1998-2002,* stresses the signifi-cance of maintaining a healthy return on capital. The report's English summary says it is important "that the labour income ra-tio is maintained at a level of around 80 percent in the coming years" (SER 1998, 9).

As in Ireland, bad times were credited with creating a new sense of reality:

> Why did the Netherlands turn the corner ahead of the rest of Europe? Three factors explain this: [1] The con-siderable shock to Dutch society of the severe economic recession in the early 1980s, when the budget deficit and unemployment boomed and the old Dutch occupation of making profit threatened to disappear: at the time the situ-ation in the Netherlands ran far more out of control than elsewhere. [2] The greater openness of the Dutch economy, which meant the Netherlands felt the cold winds of international competition sooner than many other Eu-ropean countries .... [3] The ability of the Dutch consulta-tive economy to change ..., despite the fact it had moved in completely the wrong direction for 10 or 15 years ... (VNO-NCW 1997b, 20)

But hopes for the Wassenaar agreement were low. Instead of a nationwide pact which could be used to enforce wage moderation throughout the economy, the Wassenaar agreement devolved bargaining to the local level, where wage moderation was to be negotiated between employers and employees rather than set by national negotiations, as had been the case while the corporatist model was functioning well during the 1950s. Wassenaar and future national pacts, in effect, provided broad guidelines, while specific wage agreements were worked out on the sectoral level.

The Wassenaar agreement may have been a surprise. The fact that it worked, at least to some extent, was an even greater surprise. About two-thirds of all collective agreements were renewed within two years. By 1985, fully paid cost-of-living clauses – a prime cause of the wage explosion – had disappeared from all but 10 per cent of labour agreements. Average real wages fell by 9 per cent (Visser & Hemerijck 1997, 101; N.B., chart 3-7, as well as other charts of compensation statistics, covers only manufacturing wages[4]).

In exchange for wage restraint, the unions negotiated agreements to reduce the working week in order to share work, or at least got the employers to agree to talk about shortening the work week. Yet the Wassenaar agreement remains the foundation of all further, and more successful, attempts to revitalize the Dutch economy.

> All considered, the "wage moderation for jobs" approach pioneered in the Wassenaar agreement may have been the single most important element of the "Dutch model". It ensured pay restraint and social peace, with Dutch wages

---

4. Manufacturing wages should be taken only as a loose proxy for wages through the economy. The Dutch, like other nations, have shed manufacturing employment, and the remaining jobs tend to be high-wage jobs. The numbers also do not reflect the opening of the Dutch economy to jobs in the service sector which have arisen due to wage moderation, increasingly flexibility in the Dutch labour market, and the late entrance of women into the labour market. The pool for these jobs has also been increased by stricter administration of social programmes and benefit reductions, which have made such employment more desirable.

increasing less than in partner countries on average, and the Netherlands losing proportionately fewer days to strikes than any other European country. This set in motion a "virtuous circle" of good international competitiveness, high profitability, strong investment and rapid job creation, with feedback effects on household confidence, asset prices and private consumption. ... Tax relief has underpinned disposable income, making wage moderation more acceptable, and reduced non-wage labour costs. (OECD 1998, 41)

Also in 1982, a new government was elected. Led by Ruud Lubbers, it was committed to getting public finances in order. Lubbers "started as head of government in the Netherlands with a severe and unpopular austerity policy.... [Yet] Lubbers became the longest ruling prime minister in the Netherlands, and resigned only in 1994" (CPB 1997, 83). The Lubbers government immediately froze public-service salaries, social benefits, and the minimum wage. In the spring of 1983, it went further. It announced it would cut public-service salaries, minimum wages, and social benefits by 3.5 per cent across the board. The public-sector unions organized their biggest strike since the war, but, lacking public support, they eventually settled for a 3-per-cent wage cut and a commitment to reduce the working week to 38 hours in 1986.

Government cut-backs succeeded in reducing expenditures as a percentage of the economy from 1984 to 1986. Then, following two years of expenditure increases, the downward path was again re-established. By 1990, government expenditures had fallen from the equivalent of 57.8 per cent of GDP in 1983 to 51.7 per cent of GDP.

Things Fall Apart
Government spending started to creep up again. From 1990 to 1993, government expenditures, in part because of a recession, rose to 53.4 per cent of GDP. Trouble was also brewing in the labour arena. The late 1980s were beginning to look a lot like the

late 1970s. The consensus to trade shorter hours for jobs was falling apart. In 1986, the VHP (a union of white-collar workers) broke away from the FNV coalition to press for higher wages. Within the FNV, the public servants' union, in effect, abandoned wage restraint. Dutch real compensation, after stabilizing in the early 1980s, began to rise again. Job creation flattened, though not as badly as in the early 1980s (chart 3-11 and 3-12). And GDP growth weakened.

> By 1987 the campaign for shorter working hours was dead. A year later the will to continue wage restraint seemed exhausted. The international economic upswing between 1988 and 1991 encouraged unions to raise their aspirations and renewed membership growth helped restore confidence. (Visser & Hemerijck 1997, 104)

This clearly shows the fragility of the corporatist model, when lessons so recently learned can be so quickly forgotten. It also highlights the fact that the Dutch miracle itself is not a model but rather a set of policy possibilities within the corporatist setting.

BACK TO THE FUTURE

Yet the message did get through to the social partners, though only with a lag. By 1992, the Dutch economy was in recession. A number of firms, including the giant electronics firm Philips and aircraft manufacturer Fokker, faced serious problems. One-tenth of the Netherlands's one million manufacturing jobs disappeared between 1992 and 1994 (Visser & Hemerijck 1997, 105).

The unions expressed a willingness to return to wage restraint, but the government was impatient. In 1992 and 1993, the government threatened to impose a wage freeze. This got everyone's attention. Employers were already alarmed. They warned of tough times ahead and called for zero wage growth. Still, wage settlements continued to outpace inflation.

Yet the signs of economic damage were clearly visible. The unions and employers, in part because of the threat of govern-

Chart 3-11 Annual Rate of Change in Employment

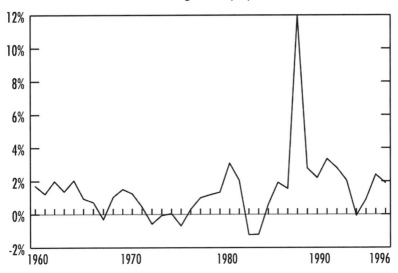

Source: U.S. Bureau of Labor Statistics

Chart 3-12 Civilian Labour Force and Employment ('000s)

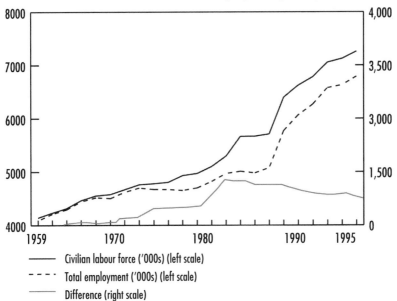

Civilian labour force ('000s) (left scale)

Total employment ('000s) (left scale)

Difference (right scale)

Source: U.S. Bureau of Labor Statistics

ment action, negotiated a two-month "breathing space" to cool down wage demands. Negotiations were suspended, expiring contracts were extended, and the social partners stepped back to view the impact of the world recession and to build a perspective on the recent Dutch economic experience.

The breathing space had a surprisingly strong impact on wage settlements. After the two-month time-out, wage increases fell to less than half what they had been. In 1993, prior to the breathing space, wage settlements averaged a 4.6 per cent increase; after the breathing, the average increase fell to 2.2 per cent[5] (Visser & Hemerijck 1997, 106). The government maintained the pressure on unions and employers to hold wages down. By mid-1993, the government was preparing wage-freeze legislation for 1994. It was also examining the idea of fundamental reform to the wage-bargaining structure. In particular, the government was prepared to review key provisions from the 1937 legislation which extended agreements negotiated in one sector to workers and employers in that sector who had not participated in the negotiations. Government officials began to argue that elimination of the extension provisions could bring increased flexibility to the labour market.

Just as economic bad times focus the mind, so do threats to privilege. Neither the union federation nor the employers federation, which negotiate the centralized agreements, wanted to see the position of these agreements down-graded or wage settlement taken out of their hands. That, as much as the economic difficulties, led to a joint defence of the extension provisions and to a new labour-management agreement, *A New Course: Agenda for Collective Bargaining in 1994,* signed in December 1993 and brought into effect in 1994. Although the extension provisions remained active, wage negotiations were further decentralized under this agreement. And, as in 1982, the unions accepted wage moderation in exchange for shorter working hours.

The impact on wages of the *New Course* was substantial. Even before the agreement was negotiated, increases in wage settlements

---

5. This is calculated on the change between agreements on an annual basis, regardless of when the agreement took effect.

Chart 3-13 Average Negotiated Wage Increases

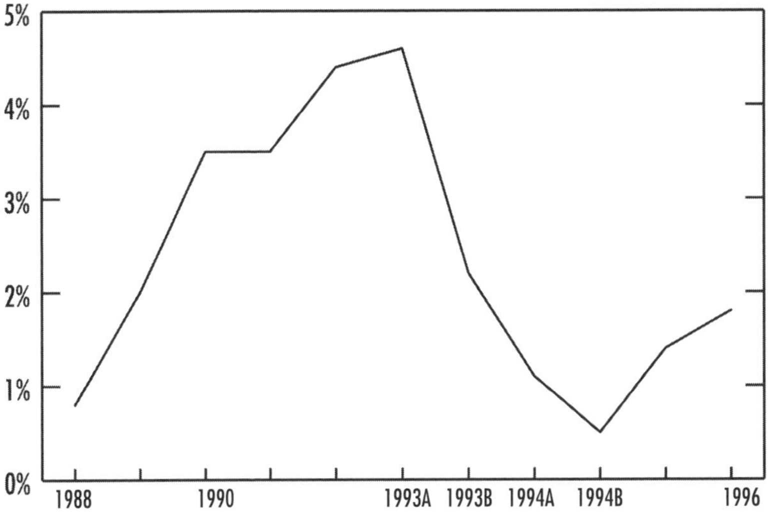

1993A: before 'breathing space'; 1993B: after 'breathing space'   Source: Visser & Hemerijck
1994A: before 'new course'; 1994B: after 'new course'   (1997, 106)

had continued to fall. As noted earlier, following the "breathing space", negotiated wage increases had fallen from 4.6 per cent to 2.2 per cent. Even prior to the implementation of the *New Course* agreement, wage increases in early 1994 had been again halved, to 1.1 per cent. After *New Course*, they were halved again, to 0.5 per cent. Wage moderation continued. In 1995 and 1996, wage settlements averaged increases of 1.4 per cent and 1.8 per cent respectively (chart 3-13).

Yet, over the longer term, as was the case in Ireland, *real* wages were boosted by wage moderation. Dutch real wages declined at the end of the 1970s and early 1980s. They began to rise again after Wassenaar, until wage moderation began to deteriorate in the late 1980s and early 1990s, which itself fed back into union militancy. But, after wage moderation was once again established in 1993-94, real wages resumed their upward course (chart 3-1).

Government Changes Direction
Consensus on holding down costs in the Dutch economy had again

been re-established. Nothing demonstrates this better than the government which emerged out of the 1994 elections. It was the Netherlands's first right–left coalition, named the purple coalition for the mixture of its blue and red political elements. The new prime minister was Wim Kok, whom we met before as the FNV leader who negotiated the Accord of Wassenaar. For a coalition headed by a former labour leader, the government launched a remarkable series of reforms. These reforms were designed to cut government expenditures, reduce taxes, increase market forces in the Dutch economy, lower regulation, and reform the welfare/social system to move people off dependence and into the work force. Further privatization, including large chunks of the social-security system, was also part of the new government's agenda.

All of these policies would, in effect, lower costs in the Dutch economy

- by reducing government spending and ultimately taxes
- by increasing the active labour pool though social program reform, thus reducing pressure on wages
- through de-regulation, and
- by reducing uncertainty related to the government expenditures, future taxation and inflation.

These measures, combined with the new consensus in labour–management relations to moderate wage costs – signified by the *New Course* agreement – led to the "Dutch miracle", as it is known today.

The Ministry of Economic Affairs report on bench-marking the competitiveness of the Dutch economy stresses the importance of a competitive fiscal structure in today's global economy:

[T]ax bases – consumption, income and capital – are increasingly mobile. The responses evoked by fiscal policy will become even stronger in the future. Relative advantages in the fiscal infrastructure will be exploited even

more, and weaknesses punished more heavily. As a result, the fiscal infrastructure will increasingly become an
autonomous factor in decisions on investment, saving,
consumption, work and domicile.... Since the government
will lose its grip on tax bases, a country's prosperity and
employment opportunities will increasingly come to depend on the "attractiveness" of the fiscal policy in that
country compared with competing countries. Even more
than before, the structure of the tax and social insurance
contribution system will have to be examined in light of
its implications for the labour market, capital market, and
competitiveness and adaptability. (Netherlands 1997, 47)

The government pledged it would cut central government expenditures by 6 per cent between 1994 and 1998. Savings would
be used to reduce the deficit and lower taxes. The government
budgeted conservatively, mindful of the fact that previous attempts
to bring the deficit under control had floundered when economic
projections proved overly optimistic.

But economic growth, spurred by the reforms and new labour
attitude, was a percentage point higher than anticipated. Between
1994 and 1995, GDP growth averaged 3.25 per cent a year (VNO-
NCW 1997a). This started a virtuous circle and enabled the government to bring the deficit down to 2 per cent of GDP in 1996
and 0.9 per cent in 1997. It has remained under 1 per cent of GDP
(*Dutch Economic Indicators*, various issues, 1998 and 1999). Economic growth helped in bringing this ratio down both by increasing revenues and by increasing the size of the divisor. Similarly,
the debt ratio was projected to drop from 77.2 per cent of GDP in
1996 to about 70 per cent in 1998.

The government exceeded its target tax reduction, cutting taxes
by 20 billion guilders (about $1.4 billion Canadian, or just over
$1 billion U.S.), about 2.5 per cent of GDP, twice the amount
promised. According to the World Bank Development Indicators
(1997), tax revenues fell from 46.1 per cent of GDP in 1993 to
42.9 per cent in 1995 (chart 3-14). The VNO-NCW (1997a), the

Chart 3-14 Dutch Government Revenue and Expenditure (% of GDP)

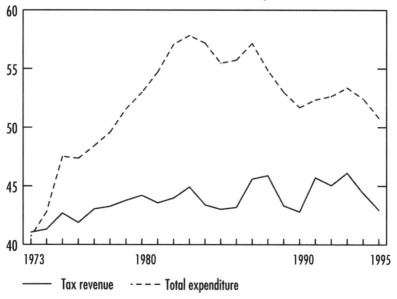

Source: World Development Indicators (World Bank 1997)

source of the statistics in this paragraph, projects the tax take will decline to 42.5 per cent of GDP in 1998, the lowest level in nearly a quarter-century. Yet, as in Ireland, over the longer term, tax cuts only increased revenues as increased GDP growth more than made up for the reductions. Statistics Netherlands (August 1999) estimates that revenues grew by 8.8 per cent in 1998 alone.

The impact of tax cuts through the whole period should not be understated in considering the Netherlands's improved cost competitiveness. To understand the impact of tax reductions, they must be put in a comparative context. In the Netherlands, the average tax burden decreased by 2.8 per cent between 1982 and 1997. Although Ireland, one of the smallest European nations, reduced its taxes after 1987, the only large European economy that achieved tax reduction was the United Kingdom, and its tax-cutting performance did not match the Netherlands's. Between 1982 and 1997, the U.K. tax burden fell by 1.9 per cent. On the other hand, the German tax burden increased by 2.6 per cent and the French tax burden by 2.3 per cent. Overall, the average tax increase across the European Union was 2.6 per cent. This alone goes a long way in explaining the Netherlands's strong economic and employment growth. Similarly, it helps explain why Ireland and the United Kingdom also stand out from other European countries in job creation and economic growth.

The Netherlands also saw a decline in the tax wedge – that is, the difference between what employees earn and what they take home after taxes. The pattern is similar to the overall tax burden. While Ireland also reduced its tax wedge, once again only the United Kingdom among the major European nations succeeded in lowering its average tax wedge, but less than in the Netherlands, 0.5 per cent compared to 4.7 per cent in the Netherlands. Again, Germany and France increased their tax wedge, by 1.2 per cent and 4.7 per cent respectively (VNO-NCW 1997b, 14).

Reducing the tax wedge, particularly at the lower end of the scale, is a key to getting people back into the labour market in the Netherlands, as in Ireland. This is captured by the SER's 1998 recommendations to government: "In the Council's opinion, an important task of the next government will be to make low-skilled work more attractive, in particular by further reducing the tax wedge between labour costs and the net wage" (SER 1998, 13).

The 1994–98 government also made efforts to get social spending under control. The Sickness Benefits Act was privatized in 1996 to remove perverse incentives in the system. Prior to 1994, sickness benefits were paid out of a large public scheme. Employers had little incentive to ensure employees did not abuse the system, since the scheme, not the employer, picked up the cost. In 1990, over seven out of every hundred working days in the Netherlands was lost to sickness leave. That compared to 2.6 days in the United Kingdom and five days in Germany (OECD 1998, 90). In 1994, small firms were required to continue paying wages during the first two weeks of sickness; large firms for six weeks, creating an incentive for firms to reduce abuse of the system.

In 1996, the system was privatized. Employers were required

to continue paying wages for the first year of an employee's sickness. Employers may either cover those costs directly or take out insurance from a private company. As with auto insurance, the cost of this insurance increases with the amount of insurance payout. Thus, whether companies pay the costs themselves or take out insurance, they have an incentive to reduce sickness leave. This is not merely a punitive measure. To reduce sick and disability leave, employers have increased incentives to keep employees healthy and happy at their work. Between 1994 and the end of 1997, absenteeism fell by 25 per cent.

After a year on sickness leave, employees are shifted to another programme, the State Disability Scheme (WAO). Here, immense problems have built up. For years, employers in the Netherlands had a perverse incentive to move redundant or poorly performing employees to the WAO permanently. Firing or laying-off employees can be exceedingly expensive under the Dutch system. The state-funded WAO provided a free way out for employers. Provided the employee claimed to be disabled, regardless of the reason, acceptance by the WAO, until fairly recently, was routine.

Employees too could initiate this action. Those in low-paid or unsatisfying jobs or employees near retirement had an incentive to move to the disability rolls or into early retirement. They were provided an income with no pressure to return to work. And, because of the high level of payments and the Dutch tax system, the difference between disability pay and work-related income could be quite small. By the early 1990s, the Netherlands – one of the healthiest nations on the planet – had 1 million of its 6 million workers classified as disabled.

The numbers have been reduced through tighter screening – at one point the sole effective criteria for disability was a claim to be disabled – and a reduction in pay-out which makes the scheme less attractive. As of early 1998, the government was planning further reforms of the WAO to create something like a standard insurance scheme, leading to further privatization. Under the proposed single disability scheme, employers will be charged insurance-like fees, which will be pro-rated by risk of disability in individual companies, based on costs related to employees' first five years of disability leave. Companies can opt out from the pro-rated premium scheme if they agree to cover the costs of disabled employees themselves for the first five years of eligibility either directly or through a private insurer. This, of course, gives employers an incentive to encourage employees to continue working. After five years, employees would be transferred to a national disability system financed by a uniform premium.

Still large problems remain. As disability qualifications were tightened, increasing numbers of Dutch workers entered early retirement schemes, once designed to open employment for younger workers. Now that the government has moved to restrict early retirement, pressure is building on the unemployment insurance scheme. Despite the pressure on these social assistance programs, Dutch companies now face a shortage of workers, including less skilled workers. A recent survey revealed that two-thirds of Dutch companies have difficulties finding staff (VNO-NCW 1997a, 34).

Economic-development Policy

Economic-development policy was changed through the period under discussion. In the 1970s, the government got into the business of protecting failing industries. This is politically tempting. Politicians and governments have a strong incentive to attempt to save existing job and industries, which have an existing political constituency. The resulting distortions may damage growth in other sectors through a misallocation of resources, but these are the yet-to-be-created, unknown jobs with no existing constituency. Because of the political dividends, subsidies to floundering industries are halted only when failure is too apparent to ignore. By the late 1970s, the failure of this policy was clearly evident in the Netherlands.

Government also faces the temptation to pick winners, since it may assume credit for the resulting jobs. Dutch industrial policy in the 1980s shifted from subsidizing declining industries to directing subsidies to industries the government decided were strong growth candidates. In other words, the government got into the business of "picking winners" and rewarding its choices with government help.

The conceptual support for this is found in the idea of market failure. The market may simply not be willing to provide appropriate amounts of capital to new economic activity. Moreover, the market will undervalue, and therefore underfund, many worthwhile activities because of externalities. Market participants will only finance activities in response to potential gains the investor can realize. But many forms of investment have strong positive externalities. In other words, the economy and society gain benefits not captured by the investor. Thus, the argument goes, society, through the government, should play a role in funding these activities in order to benefit from the externalities they produce.

Whether or not these assumptions are correct and whether or not the policy produces benefits can be judged from the outcome of these policies. As it turns out, the Dutch decided private investors, putting up their own money, are far more effective at spotting opportunities than the government. Government bodies have little history, in the Netherlands or elsewhere, of effectively picking winners. Moreover, government support for apparent winners may only weaken growth, by misallocating resources. The Dutch found that the best road to development is found by creating market conditions were the most successful companies can flourish without the diversion of resources caused by concerns about seeking government support, or the risk that a government-favoured competitor could undermine the market. Interestingly, the reduction of active, subsidy-style economic-development programmes was part of the reform package which led to stronger growth in other jurisdictions examined in this book.

The Dutch industrial policy went through these phases, with the best economic results occurring after the idea of an active economic-development policy had been abandoned.

After 1982, the government decided it could no longer

step in to rescue loss-making enterprises as she used to in the seventies.... In the eighties industrial policy changed from supporting losers to picking winners. Special attention was given to specific fields of technologies that were thought to be the most promising and rewarding ones for the Dutch economy. However in the nineties government changed that attention towards a far more generic and market driven approach: A move from "picking the winners" to "let the market pick the winners." (Klaver 1997, 8)

The CPB – in comparing Germany and the Netherlands – broadens the argument against all but the most cautious of government economic-development intervention:

[G]overnment intervention does not constitute an universal remedy [to market failure]. On the contrary, recent insights emphasize government failure and state that in some case government intervention may even aggravate market failure. ... Because it lacks price signals, the government may have less information than the market, which may make the consequences of government failure worse than those of market failure .... In other words, in these cases the transaction costs of government intervention outweigh the costs of market coordination. Government intervention may generate transaction costs through the potentially high costs of gathering information by the government, through rent seeking behaviour by the private sector and through compliance costs. Rent seeking brings about social costs when agents engage in unproductive activities to capture artificial rents created by government policies. (CPB 1997, 54-55)

The Dutch negative experience with economic-development programmes has led to a change in attitudes. "Company closures of loss-making activities are now much better understood and accepted by trade unions, the public and politicians than they were during the 1970s" (Klaver 1997, 5).

Market Reforms

In the mid- and late 1990s, the Dutch government launched a series of market reforms: a programme of privatization of government corporations, deregulation, and moves to encourage competition. The postal system has been privatized, and the monopoly on delivering printed material and letters ended. The telecom market is being partially deregulated and privatized. Two new national telephone operators were allowed to enter the market in 1997. Regulations on store hours were liberalized in mid-1996. A new competition act prohibits arrangements between companies that inhibit competition. Market dominance by an individual firm or group of firms is also restricted under the new act. The SER urges the government to go further in these areas:

> [T]he Council calls in the first place, for a further reduction in red tape for companies and individuals, also bearing in mind the burden imposed by obligations towards local governments. The next government should formulate specific targets for the reduction of red tape. Secondly, the Council refers to the introduction of competition in (quasi) public sectors ... effective competition does not come about by itself and it is above all essential to avoid replacing public monopolies with private ones. The Council further stresses the need to strive for increased effectiveness and efficiency in the performance of public tasks by making proper use of the market as an instrument. ... Thirdly, the Council refers to the "Market and Government" project, which is designed to ensure that through a clear separation of public tasks and market activities private companies do not suffer unfair competition from organisations with public tasks which operate in the market. The Council affirms this goal and calls for careful step-by-step implementation. (SER 1998, 14)

The Dutch Ministry of Economic Affairs claims the weight of Dutch regulation – as measured in five key sectors (electricity, aviation, road transport, telecommunications, and distribution) – reduces Dutch GDP by about 4 per cent.[6] The ministry turns to Sweden, of all places, to trumpet the benefits of privatization and deregulation. Swedish public transport was deregulated and partially opened to competition in 1989. By 1993, unit product costs had fallen 20 per cent. The result is particularly striking in bus transportation. According to the ministry, bus drivers in Sweden spend 70 per cent more time behind the wheel than bus drivers in Amsterdam (Netherlands 1997, 223).

THE DUTCH MIRACLE AND ASSESSMENT

By 1993–94, the Dutch economy had developed all the ingredients that would lead to the "Dutch miracle". The consensus on wage moderation had been re-established. Government expenditures were dropping. Tax relief was implemented and further relief promised. Reforms had started to the Dutch social system which were designed not just to save the government money, but also to increase flexibility and reduce wage pressure in the labour market. A promising start had begun to regulatory reform. And the government had increased its use of market mechanisms and promised further reforms. All these measures had the impact of reducing costs in the Dutch economy.

The Dutch economy responded. Economic growth was stronger than anticipated. Dutch economic indicators for December 1998 indicate a growth rate of 3.8 per cent in 1998, on top of the strong growth already discussed in the years after 1993. Inflation remained low. Prices rose by 1.4 per cent in the first 10 months of 1998, just a shade over the EU average.

Unemployment fell to 6.4 per cent in 1997. By mid-1999, it had fallen to 4 per cent. The fall in unemployment occurred even while the participation rate continued to increase, from an average of 56.3 per cent of the 15- to 64-year-old population in the first three years of the 1990s to 60.6 per cent in 1997. Employment growth has been remarkable, particularly when compared to other periods

---

6. Netherlands (1997, 214), citing *The OECD Report on Regulatory Reform* (OECD 1997).

of recent Dutch economic history. From 1985 to 1996, employment increased 39 per cent, from 4.98 million jobs to 6.92 million. Job growth has been even stronger in the post-1993 period. Between 1972 and 1983, employment increased by just under 6 per cent, from 4.67 million to 4.95 million. From 1959 to 1971, the number of jobs grew 15 per cent, from 4.1 million to 4.7 million, before declining through 1971, as the social consensus was beginning to come unravelled (chart 3-12).

Patterns and Comparisons

When the Dutch corporatist state has reached consensus on holding down costs in the economy, the Netherlands has performed remarkably well. These periods include the post-war period until the 1960s, a brief period in the early and mid-1980s, and the post-1993 period, which gave rise to the idea of a "Dutch miracle". Some economists, however, argue the Dutch success in current years is less a function of good policy now and more a function of bad policy in the 1970s and 1980s that suppressed economic growth in the Netherlands, leaving it behind the European average. Correcting the policy errors, according to these economists, simply unleashed the convergence effect for the lagging Dutch economy, speeding growth (van Ark & de Haan 1997; OECD 1998, 19-29). As noted in the previous chapter, economists have made similar observations about the Irish economy. So, as with Ireland, there are several ways to view the Dutch experience: that policy which inflates costs suppresses growth, allowing powerful catch-up growth when economic distortions are removed; or that policy which controls costs spurs unusually strong growth; or some combination of the two.

Whichever way one views the Dutch experience, it clearly shows the benefits of keeping costs in the economy under control, and it exposes the fragility of the corporatist structure. Powerful unions and a potentially interventionist government can overcome market signals, allowing wages to grow at a faster rate than economic conditions warrant. Through most of the 1970s and in the 1980s, unions pushed wages to levels that virtually eliminated profits and thus the incentive to invest and create jobs. In fact, Dutch fixed-capital formation closely follows the evolution of wages and government spending in the Netherlands (chart 3-15). It falls as wage costs and government spending rise through the 1970s. Following the Wassenaar agreement and attempts to rein in government spending, investment increases. It falls off again as costs rise in the early 1990s. Following the election of a government pledged to fiscal responsibility and the signing of the *New Course* agreement, fixed-capital formation again increases.

Job creation follows a similar pattern, though with more of a lag (charts 3-2, 3-11, and 3-12). It weakens noticeably through the 1970s, becoming negative in some years. After a brief upward blip in 1980 and 1981, job growth again turns negative. Growth turns positive and becomes strong in the late 1980s, but this leads to wage pressures and increasing wage costs. Job growth flattens in the early 1990s, before again accelerating after the 1993-94 reforms.

The same pattern is found in Dutch GDP and per capita GDP, though with two interesting twists. Dutch per capita GDP grew more slowly relative to overall GDP than was true in other European countries because of the Netherlands's strong population growth. For instance, between 1960 and 1997, Dutch population grew by 32 per cent, while German population grew by only 17 per cent (CPB 1997, 81).

Dutch per capita GDP slid against benchmark nations through most of the 1970s and the first part of the 1980s. Then growth, retrenchment, and renewed growth follow the patterns of cost movements in the Dutch economy (chart 3-16). The second interesting twist becomes apparent in examining Dutch GDP per employee (charts 3-17 and 3-18.) The same patterns are apparent, but, just as per capita GDP growth is more muted than overall GDP growth, per employee GDP growth is lower than per capita GDP growth, because the number of people employed in the Netherlands is growing faster than the population as an increased percentage of the Dutch enter the labour market and find jobs (chart 3-19).

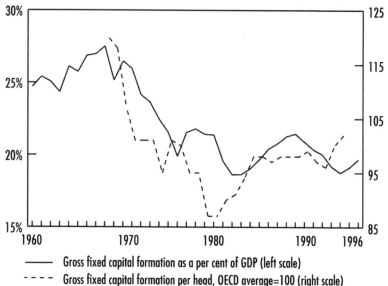

Chart 3-15 Dutch Gross Fixed Capital Formation (OECD=100)

—— Gross fixed capital formation as a per cent of GDP (left scale)
- - - - Gross fixed capital formation per head, OECD average=100 (right scale)

Source: World Development Indicators (World Bank 1997)

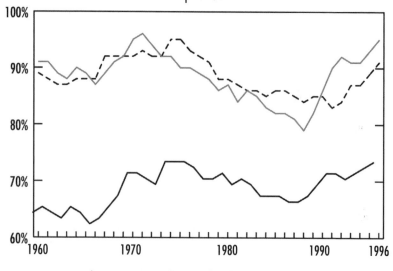

Chart 3-16 Dutch Relative Per Capita GDP

—— Dutch per capita GDP relative to United States
—— Dutch per capita GDP relative to Canada
- - - - Dutch per capita GDP relative to Germany

Source: U.S. Bureau of Labor Statistics

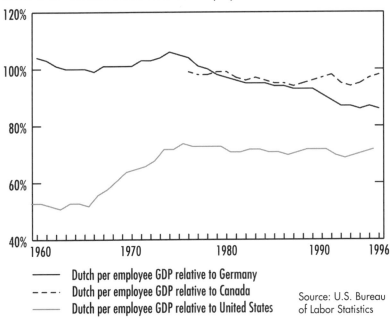

Chart 3-17 Relative Dutch GDP Per Employee

——— Dutch per employee GDP relative to Germany
– – – · Dutch per employee GDP relative to Canada
——— Dutch per employee GDP relative to United States

Source: U.S. Bureau
of Labor Statistics

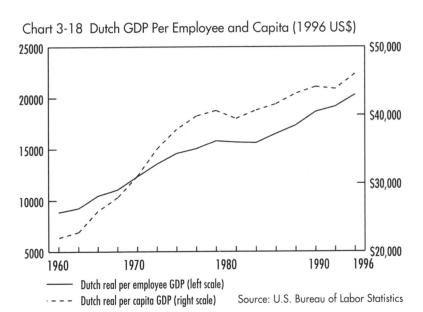

Chart 3-18 Dutch GDP Per Employee and Capita (1996 US$)

——— Dutch real per employee GDP (left scale)
· – – – Dutch real per capita GDP (right scale)

Source: U.S. Bureau of Labor Statistics

Chart 3-19   Unemployment Rate and Real Wages (1992=100)

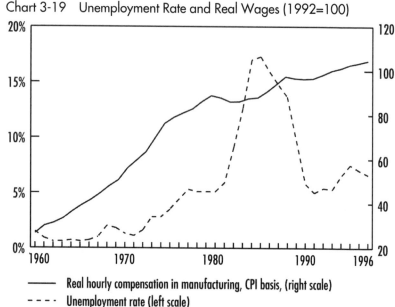

Real hourly compensation in manufacturing, CPI basis, (right scale)
- - - - Unemployment rate (left scale)

Source: U.S. Bureau of Labor Statistics

Moreover, many of the new jobs are low-productivity jobs, reflecting the increasing number of part-time and lower-skilled workers in the economy. The growth of part-time work has been a world-wide phenomenon, but it has been particularly strong in the Netherlands through the 1980s and 1990s for several reasons. The Dutch labour market has become somewhat more flexible in recent years, drawing in new participants. As well, the social pacts, which attempted to reduce the work week, opened the door to part-time workers to make up lost hours. Reforms to the minimum-wage law and social programmes increased the number of jobs and workers at the low end of the wage scale.

The most important factor, however, was the late entrance of women into the Dutch work-force. This is a relatively recent phenomenon. In a relatively short period, it boosted the number of part-time workers in the economy, something which occurred over many years, and thus more slowly, in most other advanced economies.

As the SER (1998, 3) notes in a slightly different context: "Labour productivity is still relatively high; the slower growth in recent years is partly due to a conscious choice in favour of expanding participation in the labour force, especially by those at the bottom of the labour market." One impact of the wage-moderation measures has been an opening of the Dutch service sector, where wages and productivity are routinely lower than in the manufacturing sector.[7]

Yet both Dutch policy-makers and the general population show high approval of the creation of part-time jobs. This is seen as giving workers greatly flexibility in ordering their own priorities in terms of leisure and income. It also brings flexibility to the family structure, allowing either or both parents to mix part-time work with child rearing. Finally, it reflects a late-coming change to the Dutch society and economy, the late entrance of women into the work-force. Dutch policy, especially tax policy, was focused on the single-income family. Social change, the increased openness of the Dutch economy, and changed institutional arrangements in the economy which created more flexibility for part-time work all helped boost part-time work and brought more women into the work-place. The availability of part-time and low-skill jobs also helps those entering or re-entering the work-force by providing a first job and enabling them to build skills for higher-paying work.

WILL IT LAST?

> Nowadays learning [from past mistakes] is stronger than forgetting. There may come a situation where it will be very difficult to explain to our members why we have to have a moderate wage policy. We are approaching that stage. We now have strong growth and employment is being brought back. (Cor Inja, chief labour economist for the FNV)[8]

---

7. As noted earlier, this means statistics based on manufacturing wages, as found in this chapter, understate wage moderation in the Netherlands.
8. In conversation with the author in June 1998.

A question I constantly asked in both Ireland and the Netherlands was – given the weakness of market mechanisms in setting wages and the need to maintain consensus to keep costs under control – will the Irish/Dutch miracle last? The responses were invariably pessimistic for the long term. Inja noted that, from labour's perspective, too-rapid profit growth or managers who, United States style, awarded themselves huge pay increases could cause labour's rank and file to rebel against wage moderation.

Yet, as noted earlier, a policy to increase profit margins was and is a key and explicit part of the social agreements. But there is problem with society-wide negotiations determining wealth distribution – or at least having a large say in it – rather than market forces. Who determines the proper distribution between profits and wages? Senior government officials suggest an 80/20 split in return to labour and capital is about right. Inja says his union doesn't explicitly look at profit levels but rather examines the costs producers face in other countries, as well as productivity and inflation in the Netherlands to set wage demands. The idea is not to take as much as possible in any given year – and kill the golden goose – but rather to set a fair division while maintaining the Netherlands as an attractive locale for investment and providing existing companies with the profits to generate further investment. The need for healthy profits is not questioned by the labour unions.

> We [the union movement] didn't immediately accept the relation between wages and job creation. But, you know, enterprises can't operate without a profit, and we saw big enterprises had to close their doors without a profit. We had to bring back the total number of people working. We learned [the relation between wages and profits] at a fairly late stage of the development. In the 70s, unemployment started to rise and we acted not early in 1982. You may need a crisis to achieve this understanding.[9]

---

9. In conversation with the author.

Certainly, the current generation of Dutch labour leaders not only understands the relation between job creation, moderate wage costs, and profits but are also willing to promote it vocally. Johan Stekelenburg was chairman of the FNV from 1988 to 1997 – when the federation faced some of its most difficult problems – and he successfully ran on the labour platform to become mayor of Tilburg. In 1997, he described the Dutch experience to a group of foreign journalists:

> In the past 13 years, wage costs per unit of product rose almost 30 per cent in France and even 40 per cent in Germany. Here, on the other hand, they fell by over 1 per cent! Then we have employment. Employment rose by no less than 21 per cent in the Netherlands; that's 10 times more than in France and four times more than in Germany.[10]

It is worth noting that this is a key union leader and labour politician emphasizing the relation between wage moderation and job creation, something many North American unions vocally reject. Wage moderation and, to a lesser extent, government cutbacks are almost universally credited in the Netherlands with that nation's remarkable economic and job growth.

> The Netherlands has set an example, for Europe in particular, with its low wage costs, increasingly strong competitive position and sharp rise in employment. ... The economics editors of virtually every renowned international journal and television net work travelled to Holland to view for themselves the mixture of wooden shoes, tulips and wage moderation. ... Fifteen years ago, these very same international journals and dailies told a different story. Instead of *Dutch delight* they spoke of *Dutch disease*. ... The Netherlands was cited as a prime example of

10. Quoted in van Empel (1997).

a country where growing government spending and rising wage costs had the economy in a stranglehold, causing unemployment to skyrocket. (van Empel 1997, 5)[11]

As in the Irish example, a number of factors must be counted in the mix. Efforts to reduce the tax burden have made lower wages more acceptable for union members. At the lower end of the income scale, government deregulation, greater labour-market flexibility, greater competitiveness, and reform of social programmes have created both a demand for and supply of lower-skilled workers, reducing wage pressure and creating new jobs. "The Social Partners [labour and business] have since [the early 1980s] restrained the wage development ... and contributed to a more flexible labour market. The government supported these policies by lowering taxes and social premiums, by means of reforms of the Social Security System and by a deregulation and competition drive." (VNO-NCW 1997a, 32)

Yet, because market signals are muted and can be overridden by the social partners, the corporatist model remains vulnerable, particularly when new market signals emerge but are not fully accepted by the social partners. Moreover, for the corporatist state to respond effectively to a new situation – whether changing international conditions or an internal economic boom that creates new pressures through the economy – all the social partners must come to share a common view of the situation, and this view must be *correct*. The main Dutch economic agency, the Central Planning Bureau, puts the problem succinctly and warns of the dangers ahead:

> [Corporatism] is easily made ineffective by external changes that affect the choices of the bargaining partners. This may explain why the Dutch economy was so badly hurt in the seventies, when it took a long time for the

11. It is worth pointing out that that statement is in a publication of the Labour Foundation, a joint business/labour body. The publication was signed by the co-chairs, one representing labour and the other business.

main social-economic players to regain a common view of the world. Still today, several arrangements in the Dutch institutional system lack in effectiveness, because the underlying values and norms have eroded. (CPB 1997, 541)

CONCLUSION

The Dutch and the Irish economies followed similar roads to economic ruination. Then they took strikingly similar paths to economic salvation. Outside Ireland, no one much noticed the Irish decline because Ireland *always* seemed mired in economic problems. The glimmer of hope in the 1960s had quickly been forgotten. So, to outside observers, Ireland's bleak times seemed to be nothing out of the ordinary.

But the Dutch troubles were another matter. They attracted world-wide attention, and a new phrase entered economic dictionaries, "Dutch disease". The Dutch decline was startling because the Netherlands had been one of Europe's strongest performers after World War II. Moreover, the Dutch had an energetic history, many centuries old, of wealth creation and trading vigour. This just shows how quickly even the strongest economy, regardless of the depth of its traditions, can be thrown off track.

The Dutch early post-war strategy of economic growth through cost competitiveness based on wage moderation came apart through the 1970s. At the same time, government hubris increased. Both taxes and expenditures skyrocketed. Unfortunately, expenditures had the faster take-off. The Netherlands began running huge deficits, which increased the cost of capital and costs related to uncertainty – fear of inflation and worry about high future taxes to pay off the debt. What followed was the worst period in Dutch peacetime economic history.

Slowly, through fits and starts in the 1980s and 1990s, the Dutch got their economic house back in order. Although a breakthrough labour agreement in 1982 ultimately failed in its goal of establishing durable wage moderation, further work in 1993 and 1994 succeeded in building a strong basis for moderation. Similarly, the

Dutch attack on government spending in the early 1980s faltered late in the decade. And it was never accompanied by a firm commitment to reduce taxes. The Wim Kok government, elected in 1994, changed all that, though Kok himself was the leader of the leftish Labour party. The new government forcefully tackled both expenditures and taxes. It has had considerable success in bringing both down.

It's the period after the aggressive reforms initiated in 1993 and 1994 which moderated wage growth and reduced taxes that became known as the time of the "Dutch miracle". As costs were reduced and profits restored in the Dutch economy, strong economic growth resumed. Real wages have increased. The Netherlands has gone from having one of the highest unemployment rates in Europe–not even counting the absurdly high number of people classified as disabled–to one of the lowest unemployment rates anywhere in the world. As Dutch commentators like to point out, there may be no Polder Model, but there are a lot of clear lessons to be learned from the Dutch economic experience, and economic growth is again strong.

The question is whether the lessons will be remembered or forgotten. The "Dutch miracle" has persisted only four or five years. That means it may well be premature to call this a miracle. Time will tell.

Chapter 4
Growth and Recovery in the United States

THE NATIONAL SETTING

This chapter moves from a consideration of national economies, such as Ireland and the Netherlands, to subnational economies, individual U.S. states. This limits the scope for policy action, since subnational jurisdictions obviously do not have the full array of policy tools available to nations. Thus, it is important to take a quick overview of the national policy environment in which these states operate. The occasional contrast with Canada will glance forward to the sequel, *Retreat from Growth: Atlantic Canada and the Negative Sum Economy* (McMahon 2000).

The United States has long had the world's most vibrant economy. Among the major western economies, it has the smallest government sector and, by most analysis, the least-fettered markets. Throughout the post-war period, it consistently has had the world's highest per capita GDP, with the possible exception, at times, of the United Arab Emirates.[1] Among the major nations, it also boasts the lowest unemployment rate. And it is one of the few nations that lack significant regional programmes – that is, programmes which transfer wealth to lagging regions and use government-funded "economic development" programmes to spur growth. Yet, even prior to the Second World War, U.S. economists were reporting a convergence of regional incomes. Despite

---

1. Barro & Sala-i-Martin (1995, 1, 333-34). The reference in the book is specifically to 1990, though it is true of the bulk of the post-war years and certainly of the 1990s. Switzerland is the only advanced nation that would consistently rival U.S. per capita GDP.

the conspicuous lack of regional programmes, convergence appears to have accelerated since the end of the war.

Even economists who promote and design regional economic programs, and who argue the market cannot be left to its own devices to solve regional problems, acknowledge U.S. regional problems dissipate without any special regional effort. For example, Higgins and Savoie (1995, 188), both of whom advocate active government intervention to spur regional development, note that, in the United States, "at no time has there been a *commitment* to reducing regional disparities" (italics in the original) yet market forces themselves quickly eliminate serious regional disparities. "[T]he American faith in 'rugged individualism' and the market as instruments of regional development, in most periods, has been justified" (Higgins & Savoie 1995, 187).[2]

This should not be terribly surprising, since the U.S. economic environment maintains features that are similar to strategies the Netherlands and Ireland adopted to spark economic growth. A key similarity, surprisingly, is in the labour market. At first glance, this will seem an odd statement. After all, the Netherlands and Ireland have fairly high levels of union membership. Union power is even greater than membership numbers would imply. This is because of the structure of the corporatist state, which gives unions, in conjunction with the social partners, government and business, tremendous influence over wage settlements.

In the United States, levels of union membership are low. Unions have less power in the economy than in any other major economy, save perhaps Japan. They have no direct influence on nation-wide wage-setting and only slight indirect influence, in that, for example, a large union victory may encourage other workers to seek higher wages more aggressively, while a significant defeat, such as occurred to the air-traffic controllers in the early 1980s, may discourage worker militancy.

Weak union power is one of the reasons for the flexibility in

2. Savoie is a significant figure in Canada and took credit for designing Atlantic Canada's economic-development agency, the Atlantic Canada Opportunities Agency (ACOA), though more recently he has criticized ACOA.

the U.S. labour market. When economic conditions deteriorate, unions are less able than they are in Europe to maintain uncompetitively high wages through the economy. Thus, wages adjust more readily to economic conditions in the United States – and in individual states – than in Europe. This outcome is strikingly similar to what happened in Ireland and the Netherlands, though the structure leading to the outcome was dramatically different. In Ireland and the Netherlands, unions, business, and government worked together to bring wage inflation under control and set wage rates at a level which reflected the economy's condition. They deliberately aimed at reducing costs and increasing profits in order to spark new investment, and thus economic growth and job generation.

In the United States, as we shall see, this process of wage adjustment naturally occurs through markets. Thus, if a state or regional economy experiences economic difficulties and increasing levels of unemployment, wages tend downward relative to the national average. This opens new profit opportunities and attracts new investment. Thus, it is unsurprising that regional recessions tend to be relatively brief and that lagging regions show strong convergence. Lower wage rates draw in additional economic activity. However, labour-market regulations are not identical in every state. Southern states, for example, tend to be right-to-work states, which further weakens union power and increases the flexibility of the labour-market.[3] This has been one of the reasons Southern economic growth has exceeded average U.S. economic and employment growth. And, counter-intuitively, it is also one of the reasons wage growth in the South exceeded the national rate of growth.

Because flexible labour markets tend to adjust quickly, regional recessions in the United States are usually short-lived affairs. This sets off the U.S. situation from the European environment. In Europe, militant unions or a breakdown in the corporatist state can maintain artificially high wages for a long time, even in the

---

3. See Chapter 1 for a discussion of the impact of right-to-work laws.

face of rapidly rising unemployment and falling economic activity. Thus, as happened in the Netherlands, a national recession can last many years. We'll have an opportunity in *Retreat from Growth* to view a truly perverse policy package in Canada that had the impact of artificially inflating wages in a lagging region, namely Atlantic Canada.

The other similarity between the U.S. environment and the strategies adopted in Ireland and the Netherlands involves taxes. Policy-makers in the Netherlands, and even more firmly in Ireland, slashed taxes to spur growth. The United States, on the other hand, is a low-tax environment. This, once again, allows faster economic adjustment. Nonetheless, individual states can use their own tax codes to spur increased economic growth when they face hard times. As we shall see, this was an essential element in the remarkable economic recoveries in Massachusetts and Michigan. The South, as a lagging region, has long used low state taxes to attract investment and generate jobs.

Convergence in the United States

Barro and Sala-i-Martin (1995) use a number of sophisticated techniques to test the hypothesis that regional and state economies within the United States converge.

> The main conclusion is that the U.S. states tend to converge at a speed of about two percent per year. Averages for the four consensus regions converge at a rate that is similar to that for states within regions. If we hold constant measures of structural shocks, then we cannot reject the hypotheses that the speed of convergence is stable over time. (392)

A couple of things are worth noting about this statement. First, roughly the same level of convergence is found in the other geographic areas Barro and Sala-i-Martin examine, specifically European regions and Japanese prefectures.

The second point to make, one discussed in Chapter 1, is that in their discussion of government policy, Barro and Sala-i-Martin note that growth – and therefore convergence – can be heavily affected by policy. They highlight high government consumption and taxation as negative factors in growth while positive factors include "perhaps spending on some form of public infrastructure" (1995, 7-8) and educational expenditures (1995, 433). Given that government consumption and taxation are a negative while some government expenditures are a positive, the key is obviously to focus on limited, well-directed government expenditures. Clearly while the education and infrastructure system in the United States are comparable to Canada's, overall tax rates and government consumption are much lower because of lower expenditures.

So this is the puzzle we will examine in this chapter, as we look at five states: Georgia, Massachusetts, Michigan, Louisiana, and Maine. While we in Canada have entrenched regional problems, why is it that in the United States – no matter how far a region falls, no matter how high unemployment soars, no matter how unique the problems – regional economies keep booming back? Why have regional disparities, even those with deep historic roots, faded even in the absence of government programmes designed to make them fade while in Canada regional problems seem entrenched despite, or because of, massive programs meant to eliminate them?

The opening paragraphs in this chapter sketched part of the answer. Yet the results on convergence, globally and in the United States in particular, might appear to be surprising, given the number of theories that have been developed to explain why regional economies won't converge without persistent and heroic government intervention. These theories have been used to create expensive regional programmes and bureaucracies in Canada and, to a lesser extent, Europe. The results on convergence do not seem well understood in these bureaucracies.

Convergence in the United States may be even more surprising, considering the lack of homogeneity across the nation. Resource endowments vary from extraordinarily rich to virtually non-existent, while climate varies from tropical to northern. Not only does the history of the different regions vary considerably, each region's modern economic history has a different starting point. According to many regional-development theories, these differences should have inhibited convergence without government programmes designed to combat them. Barro and Sala-i-Martin, in a number of places, note the need for homogeneity within a region for convergence to take place. But they focus on homogeneity in tastes, technology, and government policy and institutions. These are hardly identical across the United States, but they are "similar" in the broad sense used by Barro and Sala-i-Martin.

U.S. Military Spending as a Regional-development Programme

It became common for Canadian economists – and even some U.S. economists – to attribute convergence in the United States to an unofficial regional-development programme, the military. The idea was that long-serving senators and congressional representatives, particularly from the South, were able to direct a disproportionate amount of military spending to "have-not" regions. A rich proliferation of military bases and facilities helped equalize income and sparked economic growth. If this view were correct, Canada would do well to drop all regional-development programmes and start building a bigger military.

That would be pointless, for this interpretation of U.S. regional economic history is poorly researched. It collapses under any sort of empirical scrutiny. As Wright (1986, 261) shows, the Southern states have received a slightly disproportionately small share of federal spending. Slightly higher direct military spending, in some, not all, Southern states, was offset by lower spending in other areas (Weinstein & Firestine 1978, 29-43). Moreover, the South received an even lower share of federal spending during its fastest period of development. In 1952, per capita federal expenditures in the South (Georgia numbers in brackets) were only 83 per cent (77 per cent) of the national average; in 1959–61, they were 88 per cent (91 per cent); in 1969–71, 96 per cent (105 per cent); and in 1974-76, 97 per cent (94 per cent) (Wright 1986, 261).

The Southern states were also well below the national average in military contracting, which presumably should have created greater spin-offs – through plants, diversification, research, and subcontracting – than direct military spending. In fact, military contracting has been disproportionately centred in California and New England, particularly Massachusetts and Connecticut. An examination of both direct military spending and spending on military contracts clarifies the picture. In 1976, federal outlays on defence salaries averaged $139.17 per capita across the United States. They were high in Georgia, at $213.28, and low in Massachusetts, at $58.04. The mirror image of this picture emerges when one examines federal outlays on defence contractors. The national per capita average was $213.24. Georgia was well below this average, at $129.23. Massachusetts received $346.61 on a per capita basis. (California received $446.25.)

Adding the two together, Georgia received a total of $342.51 per capita in military spending, a whole dime per person above the national average of $342.41. Massachusetts received $404.65, bu California emerged as an even bigger winner, at $646.51 per person. The gross amount of federal spending tells the same story: in 1975, the federal government spent $1,454 per capita in the South Atlantic states and $1,377 per capita in the East South Central states, compared to a national average of $1,412 per capita. (All numbers in this and the preceding paragraph are from Weinstein & Firestine (1978, 31-35)).

In other words, nothing about federal spending patterns, particularly military-spending patterns, in the United States can be interpreted as a regional programme by stealth. This is particularly obvious when considering the case of California and New England, both winners, unlike the Southern states, in overall military spending. Yet these were two of the more prosperous of the states, even before military spending skyrocketed with the Second World War and stayed high through the Cold War. This direction of funds clearly does not suggest spending based on regional-development considerations.

In fact, federal expenditures, particularly in the military, merely show the feeble long-term effect of government spending on economic growth. When much defence spending was wound down at the end of the Cold War, both California and Massachusetts were hard hit. Many politicians predicted a secular decline in these two economies, and considerable political pressure developed for the introduction of regional programmes to help the two states. This didn't occur, but private-sector activity quickly crowded in after the shrinkage of the military–industrial complex. Both states are booming, with historic lows in unemployment, despite the massive defence-contract cuts of a few years back. Even in Canada, the same might be said. Ottawa and Halifax are the two most government-dependent cities in the nation. Both were hard hit by government cut-backs. Both quickly recovered.

Regional Economic Recovery and Growth

The California–Massachusetts story points up another aspect of the U.S. phenomena. No matter how hard a region is hit by a negative economic shock, it soon bounces back. Massachusetts at the end of the 1980s suffered not just severe military cut-backs, its minicomputer industry – the centrepiece of the Massachusetts technology sector – collapsed in the face of the onslaught of personal computers and desktop workstations. What followed may have been the worst regional recession in the United States since the end of the Second World War, with soaring levels of unemployment. Now every business street in Boston seems decked with help-wanted signs.

In the early and mid-1980s, the U.S. Midwest – the heart of heavy manufacturing in the United States – was devastated by overseas competition, particularly from Japanese automobile manufacturers. It was also damaged by an emerging, world-wide economic trend, the diminution of the relative importance of the manufacturing sector, the economic life-blood of the Midwest, particularly Michigan, and the shift to the service sector. Factories across the Midwest went silent.

Just as with California and Massachusetts, many thought a long-term change had occurred and the Midwest would enter a secular decline. The term "rust belt" was coined to describe this region. Many thought this phrase vividly captured the bleakness of the region, not just the visual image of a regional landscape of rusting and abandoned plants but also by aptly describing what many thought would be the region's bleak future. But once again, the economy adjusted, and much of the Midwest is, by many measures, doing even better than during the hey-day of the heavy-industry era. And all this without the type of programmes many Canadian policy-makers believe are needed to fight regional problems.

This chapter will look at five U.S. states. Three of them are in the mainstream of what was described above. Georgia, the most successful of the Deep South states, has shrugged off its once-sleepy status to develop one of the world's most dynamic economies. Michigan and Massachusetts now boast vanishingly small unemployment and strong economic growth.

Two of the states examined are atypical. Maine shows inconsistent convergence over the last 40 years. A mid- to late-1980s boom faded quickly. Although Maine per capita economic growth has outpaced Atlantic Canada's (chart 4-1)[4], it has not consistently shown strong convergence with the rest of the United States. A couple of factors may be responsible. The disproportionately rural nature of the state may slow overall economic growth. As well, Maine taxes are unusually high, and this may inhibit growth. On the other hand, recent reports from the state indicate a surge of economic activity. Perhaps convergence has renewed.

Louisiana is the other exception. The Louisiana case should be particularly puzzling to regional economists. According to most versions of regional theory, Louisiana has everything going for it and should be a leading, not a lagging, state. Far from being in the

---

4. Maine and Atlantic Canada's GDP are translated into a common currency for this chart. Large exchange-rate fluctuations are responsible for similarly large fluctuations in relative per capita GDP. Nonetheless, each trough in relative Atlantic Canadian GDP is lower than the preceding trough. In 1977, per capita Atlantic Canadian GDP was just over 77 per cent of Maine's; in 1996, it was just under 63 per cent, about one-fifth lower.

Chart 4-1 Atlantic Canada's Per Capita GDP as a Percentage of Maine Per Capita GDP, as measured in common currency

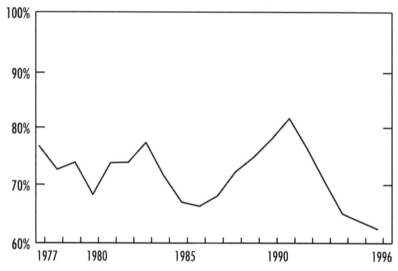

Source: StatsCan and STATS USA

hinterland, Louisiana is on one of the world's most important transportation routes and New Orleans is at its hub, near the mouth of the Mississippi River. Goods all the way from Canada flow through New Orleans and down into South and Central America. New Orleans itself has long been a major metropolitan area, still more populous than the fast-growing Atlanta, Georgia. If all that were not enough, Louisiana has huge resource wealth from Gulf of Mexico petrochemical deposits. This is hardly a resource-poor peripheral region, yet Louisiana – despite an oil and gas boom in the late 1970s and early 1980s – lags behind not just the United States but the Southeast as well.

Several factors appear to be at work in the United States that reduce regional disparities and allow depressed regional economies to regain their vigour. Strong market forces hold down costs in lagging regions and in regions suffering economic set-backs. This attracts new economic activity. Costs are not inflated in these economies, as they can be in Canada, by large wealth transfers from the central government. Lagging states, for the most part, kept their tax burden low, while governments of states in regional recessions have tended to reduce taxes to increase the competitiveness of their state. The exceptions examined here, Louisiana and Maine, have held costs high, either through relatively high taxes or government-induced cost inflation and economic distortions.

The specifics of the strategies may not perfectly fit the Canadian context. However, they have produced jobs for the people of lagging states, something that has never been successfully achieved in Atlantic Canada. And they have produced prosperity. Average wages in the once-depressed South are not merely higher than wages in Atlantic Canada; they also exceed the Canadian average.

THE SOUTH

The southern United States has long had much the same status in the United States as Atlantic Canada in Canada, as the nation's primary "have-not" region. However, unlike Atlantic Canada, where government is a central part of everyday life and economic activity, Southerners have long prided themselves on having small governments, which are expected to stay out of the everyday running of the economy. While Atlantic Canadians, for example, expect government to solve economic problems and "make" jobs, Southerners – perhaps because of their history – are deeply suspicious of government. Much of the political drive for smaller government in the United States has come from, and still comes from, the South.

The South has also promoted itself as the low-cost region of the U.S. This was particularly true of wage rates during the first post-war decades. The South has also typically had relatively low taxes compared to the rest of the United States. Weinstein and Firestine (1978, 139) note the importance of this low-tax regime:

> [T]he economic gains in the South are linked to the region's underutilized tax potential. ... [I]n 1975, state and

local governments in the South used only 82.5 per cent of their tax potential (defined as the national average tax collection rate). By contrast, the Middle Atlantic states were found to have an over-utilization rate of 10.1 per cent.

They also quote a report of the U.S. Advisory Commission on Intergovernmental Relations making a similar point:

> Both the citizens of the state and multistate corporations are more likely to perceive a heavier burden in those states where tax burdens are rising than in those states where taxes as a percentage of income are either remaining relatively constant or falling. It is that *perceived* pressure which may help to account for some of the resistance on the part of taxpayers to increase the size of the public sector and the reluctance of corporations to locate in certain areas. ... With the exception of Hawaii, California, Nevada and West Virginia, all of the states in the relatively high and rising (tax) category are in New England, the Mideast, and the Great Lakes region, while about half the Sunbelt states are in the relatively low to falling category.[5]

Charts 4-2 and 4-3 compare U.S. and Southern state taxes. This low-tax approach is, in fact, similar to the strategy Ireland and, to a lesser extent, the Netherlands have been following in recent years. On labour costs, Southern officials would also point to several factors that they claim effectively lowered the cost of labour and increased labour flexibility. These factors included low unionization, right-to-work laws, and open labour markets that featured, for example, few obstacles to laying-off or firing workers. Any examination of the economic web sites of the Southern states will show these factors still play a significant role in eco-

---

5. Weinstein and Firestine (1978, 143), quoting the Advisory Commission on Intergovernmental Relations, *Measuring the Fiscal Blood Pressure of the States, 1964-1974*, (Washington, D.C., 1977) pp. 2-3.

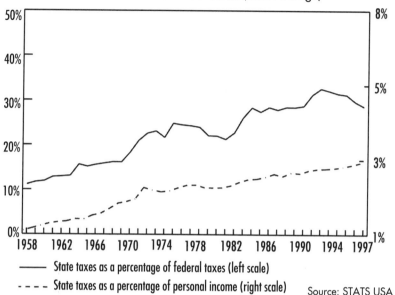

Chart 4-2 State & Local Government Taxes (U.S. Average)

——— State taxes as a percentage of federal taxes (left scale)

- - - - State taxes as a percentage of personal income (right scale)   Source: STATS USA

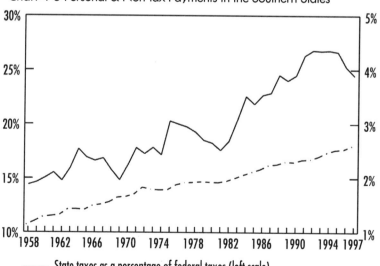

Chart 4-3 Personal & Non-tax Payments in the Southern States

——— State taxes as a percentage of federal taxes (left scale)

- - - State taxes as a percentage of personal income (right scale)   Source: STATS USA

nomic promotion. Government is seldom called on to rescue industries or create jobs. In fact, small government remains a selling point.

Is the Southern approach deeply flawed, a race to the bottom rather than a successful economic-development strategy? By virtually all measures, including personal income, the Southern economy has been a success, significantly exceeding the very strong performance of the U.S. economy as a whole. In the South, growth in personal income, average earnings per job, and per capita GDP have all consistently outpaced average U.S. growth (charts 4-4 and 4-5.)

Here again, as is the case more recently in Ireland and the Netherlands, holding wage costs down in any given year attracts investment and economic activity which leads to future wage growth as both the capital/labour ratio and human capital increase. Both factors boost the intrinsic value of labour, so that, even as wages rise, they are still relatively low compared to their return. Thus, cost-competitiveness and profits remain strong while living standards continually increase. Pay per Southern job is now almost 90 per cent of the U.S. average, but the region still boasts low wage costs because wage increases have not overtaken productivity improvements.

Although Barro and Sala-i-Martin note they cannot reject the hypothesis that the rate of convergence is constant over time, other observers believe the convergence of the southern United States is largely confined to the post-war period. Wright (1986) shows that, in 1880, the per capita income of the subregions of the South varied between 45 and 60 per cent of the national average. In 1940, they varied between 50 and 65 per cent of the national average. By 1980, the variation was from just under 80 per cent to just over 90 per cent of the national average (Wright 1986, 240).

Since 1940, per capita income in the South has persistently grown at rates well above the national average. ... [T]here was no sustained trend toward regional conver-

Chart 4-4 Southern States GSP as a Percentage of USA GSP Per Capita

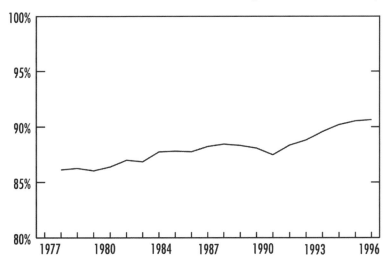

Source: STATS USA

Chart 4-5 Relative Personal Income and Earnings

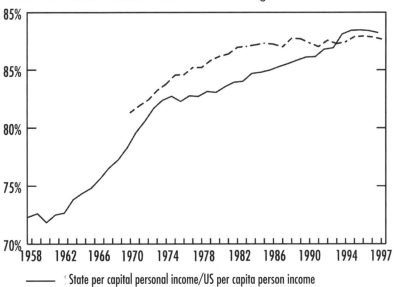

——— State per capital personal income/US per capita person income

- - - Average state earnings per job/average US earnings per job

Source: U.S. Bureau of Economic Analysis

gence before 1930. Since the modest rise during the 1930s primarily reflects the fact that the effects of the Great Depression were even greater in the North than in the South, the southern "take-off" is most appropriately dated from World War II. (Wright 1986, 239)

Two non-economic developments have helped open the South up to convergence since the end of the war. One is the invention of air-conditioning, which turned an often unbearable climate, one difficult to work in, into a desirable one. The other is the slow and difficult emergence of the civil-rights movement. While the driving force here was, as it should have been, moral, economic theory would predict large benefits from integration. It means businesses have greater opportunities because they have opened to them the full range of any jurisdiction's most important resource, its people. Integration removes any number of frictions from the labour market.

State officials and business people believe that Georgia – especially Atlanta – exhibited the least resistance of any southern state to integration, and that this provided economic benefits for the state and its capital. Roy Cooper, a retired vice-president of the Atlanta Chamber of Commerce, speaks with a perfect, slow, old-time, Southern drawl. "I'm from Birmingham originally before I came to Atlanta," he told me when I met him at the chamber's offices, "I remember when Atlanta and Birmingham – they were about the same size in the 1960s – both thought they could be the business capital of the South. But Birmingham just threw the opportunity away. They let themselves be taken up by racial problems." The Atlanta business community early on threw its weight behind the integration movement, and civic boosters coined the phrase "The City Too Busy To Hate".

Georgia

Of all the Southern states, Georgia's success is the strongest. Its per capita GDP now exceeds the national average, and pay per job is close to the national average (charts 4-6 and 4-7). Georgia

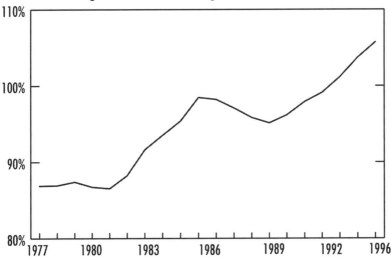

Chart 4-6 Georgia GSP as a Percentage of USA GSP Per Capita

Source: STATS USA

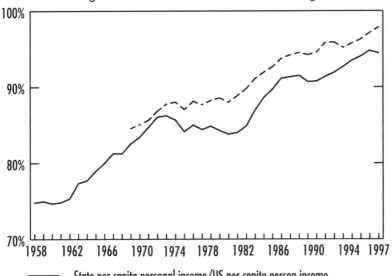

Chart 4-7 Georgia: Relative Personal Income and Earnings

———— State per capita personal income/US per capita person income

– – – – Average state earnings per job/average US earnings per job

Source: U.S. Bureau of Economic Analysis

has become such an economic power-house – one of the world's most successful and dynamic economies – that people forget that not long ago, it was a sleepy state, in the deepest of the Deep South – in a strip of three depressed states, Georgia, Alabama, and Mississippi.

Now Atlanta boasts one of the world's most glittering skylines. Many of the world's most dynamic companies are headquartered here. Tens of millions of people see pictures from Atlanta every-day on the Atlanta-based CNN. Georgia sped ahead of the rest of the United States. Georgia's economy is 150 per cent larger now than 20 years ago. The U.S. economy is only 66 per cent larger; the Canadian economy just 45 per cent larger.

This must be a great puzzle to traditional economic developers. Georgia is not a resource-rich state. Lack of resources, under many of the traditional regional-development theories, should block the acquisition of capital needed to boost economic growth. Moreover, traditional theory says, isolation from centres of economic activity should lock in backwardness, particularly in the absence of resource wealth to spark and fund investment. That argument is often used to justify regional subsidies.

Georgia was in the midst of an economic hinterland, separated by difficult geography from the industrial heartland of the United States. The state's main city was not connected by any natural transportation feature to more prosperous areas, as New Orleans was by the great Mississippi. It grew because it was at a railroad crossing. Government and business have worked hard to improve transportation links.

Traditional development theory also focuses on money. Poor regions need subsidies to bring services up to the level needed to spark economic growth. And poor regions must give subsidies to business to attract investment, which would naturally prefer to stay at the centre unless bribed away. This is even more important, the argument goes, since the capital market is thought to be imperfect and would undersupply poor regions. The Georgia story puts paid to this argument.

Georgia did not benefit from federally sponsored regional-development programmes. It could not even use traditional state-run programmes. Georgia's cranky constitution prohibits state "gratuities", which the Georgia Supreme Court has interpreted as a prohibition on subsidies to business. Georgia has a smattering of small tax-reduction programmes and programmes to provide infrastructure and training, but it simply cannot compete with neighbouring states in the subsidy game. Georgia has thus lost out on the big catches made by other Southern states, most notably large automotive investments, such as Mercedes to Alabama and Saturn to Tennessee. These packages can be hugely expensive:

> As an example of the price escalation in this [economic development] war ... Tennessee paid $11,000 for every job created at a major Nissan plant in 1980. Five years later, the state paid $26,000 per job to win the Saturn plant. More recently, South Carolina paid $71,000 per job to land the BMW plant, and Alabama paid $169,000 per job to win the Mercedes plant. (Toft 1995)

So why is Georgia doing better than these states? There is no evidence that active economic-development programmes produce economy-wide benefits. And, even when they succeed, the attracted business may simply crowd out other private-sector activity, leaving even the local community little better off, but at a significant cost to taxpayers. Finally, and most dangerously, subsidies may go to a politically connected business in competition with other business, possibly allowing a less competitive business to drive out a better-run business, leaving the economy worse off in the long run. The economy has lost a good, taxpaying business and gained a state client. Finally, such programmes can weaken the overall competitiveness of business by leading business to concentrate on rent-seeking opportunities rather than market opportunities. This dependence and misplaced effort creates another net loss to the economy.

Certainly, Georgia has not been harmed by not having direct subsidy programmes, as can be seen from charts 4-6 and 4-7.

Georgia officials like to tell visitors they can assure indigenous businesses and ones which may be considering a Georgia location that their tax dollars will never be used to subsidize a competitor and that Georgia taxes will be low for every business. That creates a level playing-field inside the state, but a competitive advantage nationally.

Typically, economic-development subsidy programmes are disproportionately directed at out-of-state enterprises. When these programmes are large, they use tax dollars raised from indigenous business to subsidize external firms. Even when these firms don't compete with local business, they have a negative impact by forcing up costs as they compete for land, labour, and other resources. Thus, Georgia's lack of subsidy programmes may have indirectly benefited indigenous businesses.

Yet indigenous firms – not outside economic stars like carmakers – are the key to economic growth. The importance of indigenous firms holds true in the southern United States. Weinstein and Firestine (1978) review the literature and find that employment growth and loss has very little to do with the in-migration and out-migration of firms "both [in] the North, where employment is growing slowly, and the South, where employment is growing rapidly. Births and expansions [of indigenous firms], by contrast, vary significantly among regions and can be cited as the major causes of differential employment growth. ... [T]he primary cause of rising employment in the Sunbelt has been the expansion of existing firms and the birth of new firms" (1978, 131, 134).

Georgia's development programmes, instead of emphasizing subsidies, focus on "soft" services, like training, and investments in infrastructure, which remain in the state even if the assisted business fails. Because money is not passed on to the company, no firm invests in Georgia to reap a subsidy. But Georgia – in a renowned and much-copied programme – will provide training for a new company's work-force, though they will not fund a company training programme. This avoids companies settling in Georgia to seek a subsidy under the guise of training. Instead, company officials tell the state what skills they need and they work with state officials in setting up the programme, which is run by the state. Whatever happens to the client company, the skill level of the work-force is improved.

Georgia will also help with infrastructure costs. But such infrastructure obviously remains in the state even if the client company leaves. And Georgia has developed a bank to provide that most necessary of all ingredients for success: information. Georgia's data bank will tell a company which locations meet its requirements – whether these are for specific transportation links, several nearby machine-tool shops, or a work-force with experience in the furniture industry. Thus, firms can find the most cost-efficient location for them in Georgia.

Labour costs in Georgia are now close to the national average. But Georgia has maintained a consistent gap between its per capita GDP and average state wages. For example, in 1996, Georgia's per capita GDP was over 105 per cent of the national level, but average Georgia wages were only about 92 per cent of the national average. This suggests that Georgia workers were somewhat underpaid or, looked at another way, that labour costs were inexpensive compared to level of output. Yet Georgia's average wages and personal income have consistently risen against the national average. This supports the idea that competitive labour costs, while, in any given year, providing workers less than their maximum possible pay, create long-term benefits for workers. It attracts more capital, increasing the capital/labour ratio and thus the pay-out to labour. New and ongoing investment and continuous employment increases the value of human capital, intrinsically increasing the value of labour and the pay-out to it.

Georgia has maintained a relatively small, inexpensive state government. Georgia state and local government employment, at about 13 per cent of total employment, is similar to the national average (chart 4-8). But state and local government as a percentage of GDP are below the national average (chart 4-9), as are Georgia state and local taxes. Only about 15 states have taxes lower than Georgia's. In 1993, state and local revenues in Georgia equalled $219 for every $1,000 of personal income; the national

Chart 4-8 Georgia: State and Local Employment as a Percentage of Total Employment

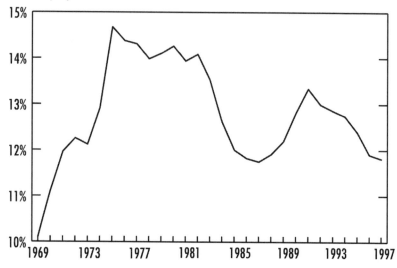

Source: U.S. Bureau of Labor Statistics

Chart 4-9 Georgia: State and Local Government as a Percentage of the National Average

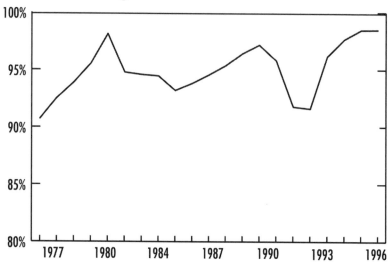

Source: STATS USA

average was $232 per $1,000 of personal income (Tan Foundation 1997; chart 4-10). Moreover, Georgia spends its money wisely. For example, Georgia has "the nation's best highway quality", according to research conducted by the independent Corporation for Enterprise Development (1996, 56).

This helps, but Georgia's most important competitive advantage is clearly in the cost of labour. The relationship between Georgia's unemployment and pay rates is not clear-cut, in part because Georgia's relative pay has been on a long-term secular rise. Nonetheless, increases in relative pay soften as Georgia's unemployment rate rises against the national average (chart 4-11).[6] Georgia has experienced strong employment and labour-force growth and shrinking levels of unemployment for the last decade and half (charts 4-12 and 4-13).

Georgia provides a road-map for success. It shows that when labour and tax costs are kept competitive, not only does the state economy grow, but wage rates also rise. It also shows that heroic government economic-development efforts are hardly necessary for success. In fact, given Georgia's record against other Southern states, which boast massive subsidy programmes, lack of such efforts appears to be quite beneficial.

Louisiana

If Louisiana is not the most blessed state in the United States, it is certainly the most blessed Southern state. New Orleans sits at the nexus of one of the world's great transportation routes. A key to

---

6. A state's unemployment rate relative to the national average should move in the opposite direction from average state earnings relative to the national average. To help visually interpret the data, I've used the U.S. employment numbers as the numerator of the first series, and U.S. average earnings as the denominator of the other series in this chart and similar charts for the other states examined. This inverts one series relative to the other, so on the chart they should move in the same direction. The blip in Georgia employment in 1991 is probably due to the Gulf War. As noted earlier, Southern states have somewhat higher concentrations of military personnel than the national average, though lower levels of defence contracting.

Chart 4-10 Georgia: State Taxes

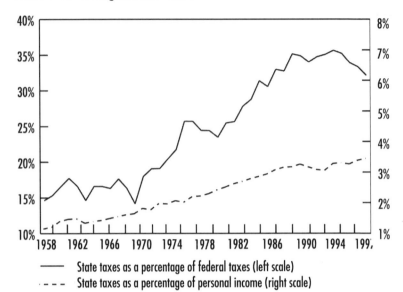

State taxes as a percentage of federal taxes (left scale)
State taxes as a percentage of personal income (right scale)

Source: STATS USA

Chart 4-11 Georgia: Unemployment and Real Wages

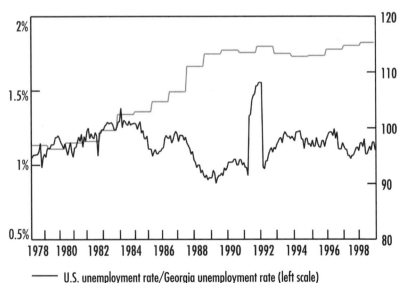

U.S. unemployment rate/Georgia unemployment rate (left scale)
Average state earnings per job/average U.S. earnings per job (right scale)

Source: U.S. Bureau of Labor Statistics

Chart 4-12 Georgia: Employment Growth

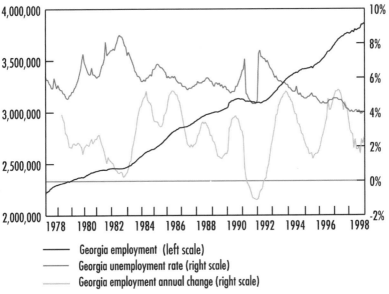

Georgia employment (left scale)
Georgia unemployment rate (right scale)
Georgia employment annual change (right scale)

Source: U.S. Bureau of Labor Statistics

Chart 4-13 Georgia: Employment and Labour Force

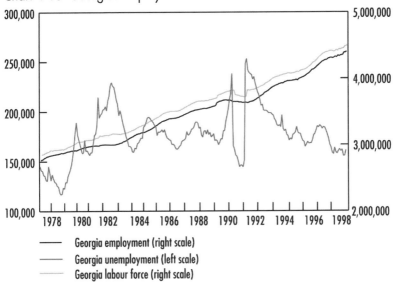

Georgia employment (right scale)
Georgia unemployment (left scale)
Georgia labour force (right scale)

Source: U.S. Bureau of Labor Statistics

economic development and growth throughout economic history has been proximity to trade routes.

Louisiana has also experienced a resource bonanza because of Gulf of Mexico petrochemical deposits. The two together – transportation routes that tie Louisiana to many major markets and resource wealth – should, by most versions of economic-development literature, push Louisiana's development into fast forward. Yet Louisiana's experience shows that resource wealth is not a recipe for real economic activity that produces sustained wealth for people, good-paying jobs, and high employment.

It also shows what a difference policy makes. While neighbouring resource-rich Texas prospers, resource-rich Louisiana's per capita GDP has fallen well behind the national average. Texans have traditionally been suspicious of big government. In Louisiana, government, at least since the days of Huey P. Long, has played a large role in the state economy and society. Louisiana, unusually for a Southern state, is a high-tax state. In 1993, state and local revenues in Louisiana equalled $262 for every $1,000 of personal income, 13 per cent above the national average of $232 per $1,000 of personal income. Only about half a dozen states collect more revenues than Louisiana. (All figures in this paragraph are from Tax Foundation (1997)).

Louisiana has a history as the South's high-tax state. In 1975, Louisiana was the only state in the South with a tax burden above the national average, though West Virginia and Mississippi, two other low-growth Southern states, were within three percentage points of the national average. All other Southern states had considerably lower burdens. Georgia's tax burden was 84 per cent of the national average, for example.

Most Southern states had higher levels of taxation, relative to the national average, in the early 1950s, but Louisiana's was a whopping 138 per cent of the national average, obviously much higher than the national average but also higher by at least 10 percentage points than any other state in the nation save North and South Dakota (Weinstein and Firestine 1978, 140-141). State

Chart 4-14 State and Local Government Employment as a Percentage of Total Employment

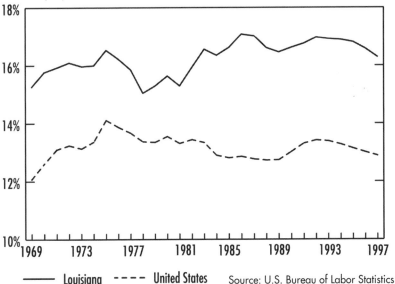

——— Louisiana   - - - - United States   Source: U.S. Bureau of Labor Statistics

and local unemployment is an unusually high percentage of total employment (chart 4-14).

Economic activity was driven to new heights in Louisiana in the late 1970s and early 1980s by the petrochemical boom. But, far from bringing any lasting benefits, this bonanza seemed to do lasting damage to Louisiana's economy. Per capita GDP, personal income, and wages all rose rapidly then fell precipitously. By the mid- to late-1980s, all had fallen to levels below where they had been, relative to national averages, prior to the boom, though personal income has recovered somewhat since 1989 (charts 4-15 and 4-16).

Average earnings were driven well above national averages, as would be expected, by the boom. The attractiveness of high-paying jobs in the petrochemical industry doubtless made it more difficult and expensive for other businesses to attract and hold labour, particularly skilled labour. Increasing state employment

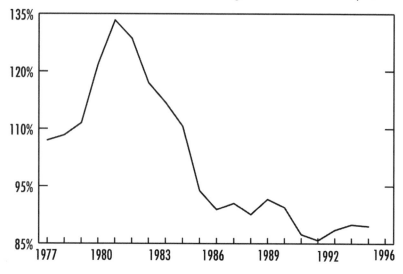

Chart 4-15 Louisiana: GSP as a Percentage of USA GDP Per Capita

Source: STATS USA

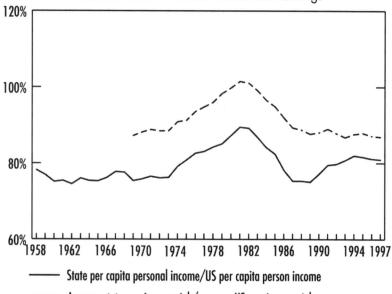

Chart 4-16 Louisiana: Relative Personal Income and Earnings

—— State per capita personal income/US per capita person income

– – – Average state earnings per job/average US earnings per job

Source: U.S. Bureau of Economic Analysis

also put upward pressure on wages, again making life more expensive for other state businesses. The impact on wages is obvious in chart 4-16. This suppressed other economic activity, and, when the petrochemical boom was over, the state economy was in worse shape than before. This is classic "Dutch disease" and shows that resource wealth, far from being the cutting edge of economic-growth strategy, is a dangerous two-edged sword.

The bloating of state government is strongly evident in chart 4-14. State and local employment start rising as a percentage of total employment with the oil crisis of the late 1970s. Nationally, the ratio is falling through this period. Because Louisiana is a resource-rich state, the oil crisis created tremendous investment and private-sector job growth in the state. By itself, this should have pushed down ratio of government workers to private-sector workers. As well, with incomes rising and unemployment falling, the need for state services should have declined.

Successful resource jurisdictions, like Texas and Alberta, use petrochemical wealth either to provide increased services at no extra cost to taxpayers or to decrease the tax load. Either strategy reduces costs and offsets the inflationary impact of petrochemical activity. Unfortunately, Louisiana chose to increase taxes. This meant non-petrochemical businesses faced both rising wage costs and higher tax bills. State personal income taxes grew dramatically as the oil boom reached and then passed its peak. At the top of the oil boom, 1981, Louisiana's state corporate-tax collections had risen to the eighth highest in the nation per $1,000 of personal income. The state government pumped itself up as well, though higher rates of economic growth and employment creations should actually have reduced state expenditures.

Although Louisiana maintained high corporate taxes and royalities, its personal taxes remained low by national standards (chart 4-17). In fact, they did decline somewhat towards the end of the oil boom, before moving upwards once again. The size of the state government as a percentage of GDP did rise against the national average during the oil boom – when the government actually should have been getting relatively smaller because of the

Chart 4-17 Louisiana: State and Local Government Taxes

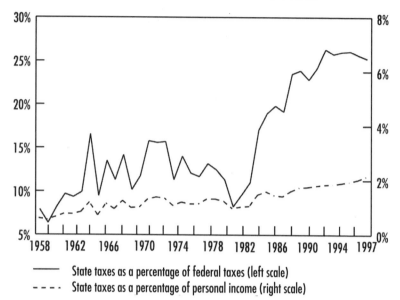

State taxes as a percentage of federal taxes (left scale)
- - - - State taxes as a percentage of personal income (right scale)

Source: STATS USA

growth of resource activities – but after the oil boom it slipped back below the national average (chart 4-18).

The problem appears to be return for these expenditures. Regardless of the level of state spending, Louisiana has always ranked low on measures of provision of services, like education and infrastructure. As the Corporation for Enterprise Development reported (1996, 72), "Louisiana's development resources are the worst in the nation. With the nation's lowest high school graduation rate, the state's Human Resources receive a failing grade." Louisiana policy-makers exhibited a lack of attention to providing key state services, particularly as government was growing through the oil boom. In 1978, prior to the boom, Louisiana's state and local government were at 91 per cent of the national average; the same GDP-based measure of spending on education was at 77 per cent of the national average. Lousiana state and local government climbed to 104 per cent of the national average in 1982;

Chart 4-18 Louisiana: State and Local Government as a Percentage of National Average

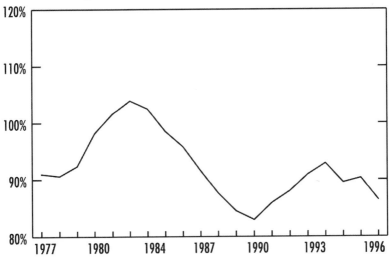

Source: STATS USA

education had fallen to 73 per cent of the national average. In 1996, state and local government had fallen to 86 per cent of the national average, education to 68 per cent. The list could go on. For example, Louisiana also rates in the bottom five states for transportation infrastructure.

It also has a widespread reputation for political spending and corruption, neither of which provide value for taxpayers' money. Although it is far beyond the scope of this book to examine closely the nature of spending during the petrochemical boom, the universal view across the state is that the money was simply frittered away in ways that may have bought votes but did not improve infrastructure, that may have rewarded powerful political friends but contributed little to education and other essential state services. I heard this view from city officials in New Orleans, from high state officials, including at the cabinet level, in Baton Rouge, and from economists – for that matter, everyone I spoke with in the state.

The lesson from the petrochemical boom seems to have been

Chart 4-19 Louisiana: Employment and Labour Force

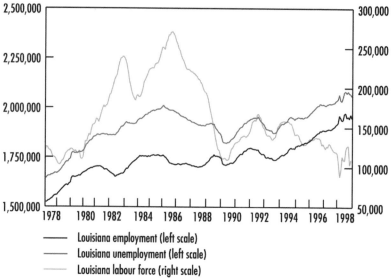

Louisiana employment (left scale)
Louisiana unemployment (left scale)
Louisiana labour force (right scale)

Source: U.S. Bureau of Labor Statistics

well absorbed in the state. The state government is working to
reduce taxes and provide better services for the money. Budget-
ary problems are being brought under control. State employment
as a percentage of the work-force has been on a slow decline since
the early 1990s. This is largely due to non–government-employ-
ment growth. State per capita GDP has at least stabilized against
the national average and, since the early 1990s, has shown some
signs of increased growth. Similarly, over the same period, employment and the labour force have grown while unemployment
has decreased (charts 4-19, 4-20, and 4-21).

Louisiana once again shows that policy matters and that states
have to be careful about their cost structure and about getting
value for money. Both locational advantage and a sudden surge
of resource wealth – like a lottery winning – can be frittered away
if policy is bad. Resource wealth can damage a state economy
instead of bringing benefits to the citizens of the state.

Chart 4-20 Louisiana: Employment Growth

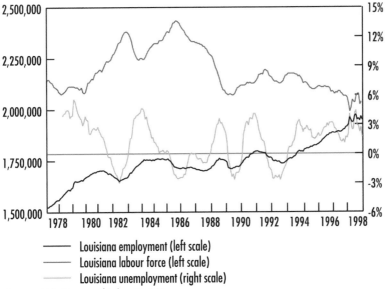

Louisiana employment (left scale)
Louisiana labour force (left scale)
Louisiana unemployment (right scale)

Source: U.S. Bureau of Labor Statistics

Chart 4-21 Louisiana: Unemployment and Earnings

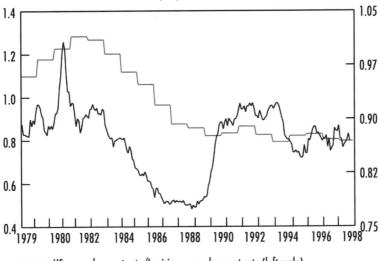

US unemployment rate/Louisiana uemployment rate (left scale)
Average state earnings per job/average US earnings per job (right scale)

Source: U.S. Bureau of Labor Statistics

MASSACHUSETTS

It was the worst of times. By the late 1980s, the Massachusetts economy had been slammed by a triple whammy – a state budget out of control, and the virtual collapse of both the state's computer and defence industries. It was, by some counts, the worst regional recession in the United States since the end of the Great Depression, and it hit about two years before the rest of the U.S. economy was affected. Unemployment soared nearly to the double-digit level, even though hundreds of thousands of people left the work-force, or simply left the state. Taxes were high; spending was higher still. The state was nearly bankrupt. Massachusetts was the hardest-hit state, but the whole of New England was in deep recession:

> New England is now [i.e. in 1994] emerging from its longest and deepest recession since the Great Depression of the 1930s. From its peak in early 1989 to its lows in the summer of 1993, the region's non-farm employment fell 10.9 %, representing the loss of 725,000 jobs. New England's recession was far more severe than the nation's – U.S. employment fell just 1.5% from mid-1990 to mid-1991 and had fully recovered by the end of 1993. Unlike the mild contraction of the 1980/82 period, this recession was experienced in every sector of the New England economy except health care. White-collar jobs became as expendable as blue-collar jobs. (DRI Canada et al.1994, 3-128)

Today, Massachusetts is booming. Taxes are down, yet the state runs a surplus. Unemployment has fallen to under four per cent, the lowest of any major state. (Canadian and U.S. unemployment rates are calculated differently. By Canadian measures, the Massachusetts unemployment rate would be about four per cent. Given that some people are always moving between jobs, this still translates into full employment in most of the state. It's hard to walk a block in any Boston business district without seeing a bevy of help-wanted signs.)

What happened? Let's look firstly at reasons for the boom. Massachusetts's large defence industry benefited mightily from the Reagan military build-up. Massachusetts receives even today about three times as many defence contracts per capita as the rest of the country, and four times as many research awards. This became a river of gold during the Reagan build-up.

The 1980s were also a time of great excitement around Massachusetts's high-tech industry. There were three reasons for this excitement: military spending contributed to it; a number of new commercial technologies were emerging from Massachusetts' institutes of higher education, particularly the Massachusetts Institute for Technology (MIT); and the minicomputer industry, largely centred in Massachusetts and led by Digital Equipment Corp. (DEC), was booming.

Chart 4-22, which shows the rise and fall of Massachusetts's electronic industry, can serve as an approximate proxy for both increased military spending and the minicomputer industry. Explosive growth is evident until 1986, when the industry began to shrink rapidly. The early growth helped power Massachusetts's economy. Per capita GDP rose strongly against the national average (chart 4-23). Employment growth was also rapid during this period, and the unemployment rate fell to around 4 per cent (charts 4-24 and 4-25).

Massachusetts's Economic Problems

Now let's look at the state's three key economic problems. The biggest was self-inflicted. The state government took credit for the "Massachusetts miracle". It started building ever-bigger state government and feeding itself through ever-higher taxes. People started calling the state "Tax-achusetts". Taxes were spectacularly raised and government enlarged just as the bloom was coming off the boom (charts 4-26 and 4-27). By 1987, state corporate taxes were the third highest in the nation (Massachusetts Taxpayers

Chart 4-22 Massachusetts: Electronic Industry on a Per Capita Basis as a
Percentage of the National Average

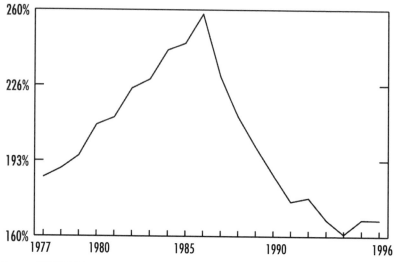

Chart 4-23 Massachusetts: GSP as a Percentage of USA GSP per capita

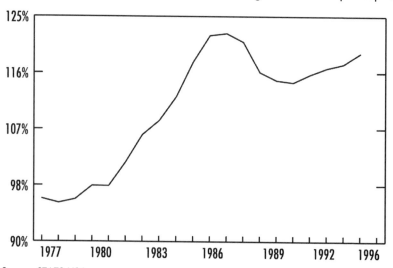

Chart 4-24 Massachusetts: Employment Growth

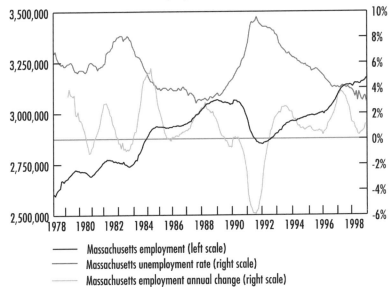

Massachusetts employment (left scale)
Massachusetts unemployment rate (right scale)
Massachusetts employment annual change (right scale)

Source: U.S. Bureau of Labor Statistics

Chart 4-25 Massachusetts: Employment and Labour Force

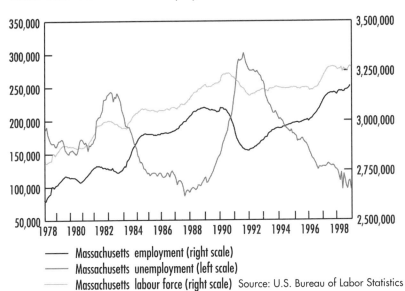

Massachusetts employment (right scale)
Massachusetts unemployment (left scale)
Massachusetts labour force (right scale) Source: U.S. Bureau of Labor Statistics

Chart 4-26 Massachusetts: State and Local Government as a Percentage of National Average

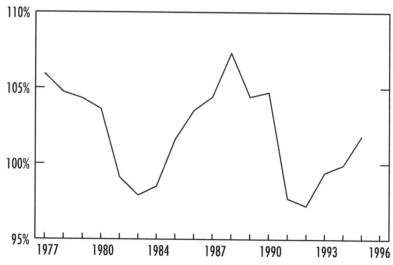

Source: STATS USA

Chart 4-27 Massachusetts: State Taxes

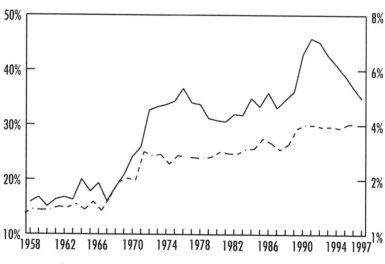

—— State taxes as a percentage of federal taxes (left scale)
- - - State taxes as a percentage of personal income (right scale)

Source: STATS USA

Chart 4-28 Massachusetts: State and Local Employment

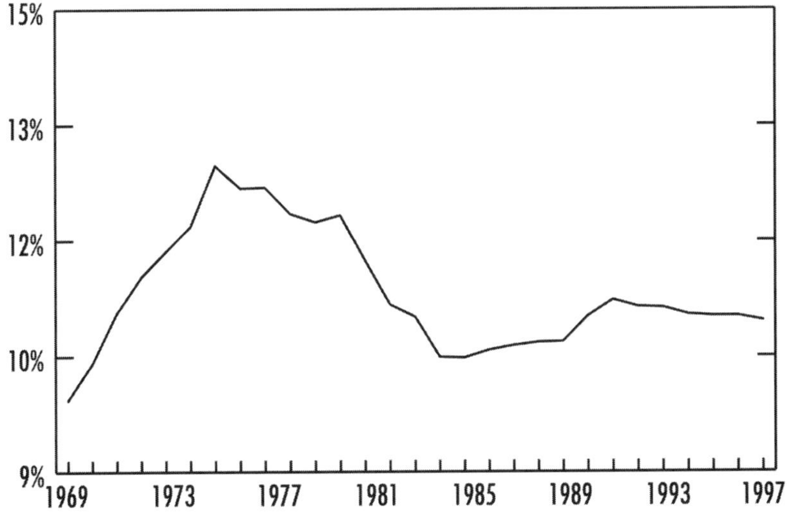

Source: U.S. Bureau of Labor Statistics

Foundation 1997). Although state and local employment as a percentage of total employment has never been particularly high in Massachusetts, it also grew through the Tax-achusetts period (chart 4-28).

Business costs soared, lifted higher by the upcurrent of a speculative bubble. This exacerbated the other two economic difficulties facing Massachusetts – the disasters that befell the huge computer and military industries.

Minicomputers had been busily pushing mainframe computers out of the office. But, towards the end of the 1980s, personal computers and workstations began to come of age, and the minicomputer industry went into a tail-spin. Much of what survived of Massachusetts's computer industry picked up and moved to the friendlier business climes of North Carolina, Texas, and, of course, California – the PC hot spot. At the same time, the Cold War was winding down. Spending cuts devastated the Massachusetts defence industry. And high taxes in Massachusetts didn't make it an attractive place for whatever defence work remained on the table.

Chart 4-29 Massachusetts: Relative Personal Income and Earnings

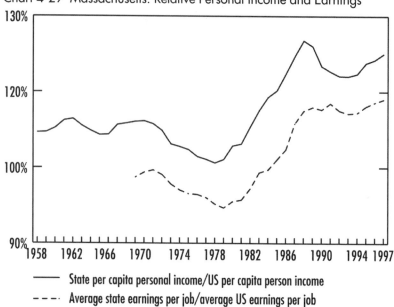

State per capita personal income/US per capita person income

----· Average state earnings per job/average US earnings per job

Source: US Bureau of Economic Analysis

As can be seen from chart 4-22, Massachusetts's electronic industry has never recovered its national pre-eminence.

Employment growth turned negative. In just two years, from 1989 to 1991, Massachusetts lost over 200,000 jobs (charts 4-24 and 4-25). Personal income, which had been driven up by the boom, now dove (chart 4-29). And relative per capita GDP also fell dramatically, as noted earlier.

If these woes hit a regional economy in Canada, we'd call on the federal government for help. We'd demand subsidies for failing industries. We'd call for make-work projects, economic-development measures, and a more activist government. If Massachusetts were a Canadian province, we'd probably still be subsidizing the mini-computer business against all odds, just as the federal government and Nova Scotia have subsidized the province's much more antique steel and coal industries.

This kind of response only papers over failure. It entrenches and artificially props up the very structures that caused the problems. But Massachusetts did the opposite. The state's heavy fall from economic grace led to a revolution in thinking. Maybe it had to. Federal regional aid is low to non-existent in the United States. U.S. regions must solve their own problems with their own resources. So Massachusetts, Michigan, California, and other depressed states adopted virtually identical policies. And had virtually identical success in halting their problems before they became entrenched.

The timing and the politics differed from state to state. In Massachusetts, for example, the legislature remained overwhelming liberal, Democratic, and sympathetic to organized labour. The socially liberal, economically conservative Republican Bill Weld became governor.

Just as in other economically troubled states, a clear consensus developed on what needed to be done: get government under control and reduce its interference in the economy. Cut expenditures and slice away at the cost of doing businesses in Massachusetts – specifically taxes. Massachusetts took a counter-intuitive approach to job creation. No one doubted Massachusetts needed jobs, but government reduced the number of state jobs. Massachusetts policy-makers understood an economy is made strong, not by spending tax dollars on make-work activity, but by allowing the private sector to create sustainable, productive jobs. Even the state economic-development department was downgraded, its budget slashed, as was the state's executive department, from 70,000 in 1994 to 54,000 in 1996.

High taxes had been slowing down real job creation. State income taxes as a percentage of federal taxes were slashed (chart 4-27). Corporate taxes were also slashed. In 1987, the state collected $11.25 in state corporate tax per $1,000 of personal income ($206 per capita) compared to a U.S. average of $5.72 ($85 per capita). In 1994, the state collected $6.83 in state corporate tax per $1,000 of personal income ($176 per capita) compared to a U.S. average of $3.95 ($109 per capita). These cut-backs enabled the state to reduce its tax burden by about eight per cent. Unemployment fell. State taxes remain relatively high in Massachusetts, but, at their present level, they are compensated for by world-class education, health care, and research facilities. While many are private institutions, almost all are supported by government money. The state also has a strong infrastructure. In other words, value is provided for tax dollars.

The government also moved to reduce regulatory costs. "Since February 1996, the administration has reviewed 1,600 regulations. As of January 1997, 22 per cent of regulations were rescinded, 49 per cent of all regulations were modified, and only 29 per cent of all regulations were retained in their existing form" (Cellucci 1997, 11).

A flexible labour market was also key to Massachusetts's recovery. When Massachusetts's unemployment rate skyrocketed, average earnings per job, as a ratio to the U.S. average, levelled off and then fell, before growing again with the state's recovery in the late 1990s (chart 4-30). Nonetheless, many economists in Massachusetts are surprised at how little average wages moved in response to the large increase in unemployment.

Labour economist Andy Sum, a professor at Northeastern University and head of the university's Center for Labor Market Studies, thinks he can solve at least part of the puzzle. He notes the state's actual job losses are far greater than the numbers that show up in the Stats USA data base on unemployment. "From the start of the Massachusetts recession to its bottom, we ... lost 568,000 jobs. Unemployment should have gone up to 14 per cent."[7] But, unemployment hit only 8 or 9 per cent, and the state employment numbers, based on a labour-force survey, show a much smaller job loss.

Several things happened to reduce the impact of job losses. Some people left Massachusetts to go where the work was; others, particularly the older and the less skilled, left the labour force. Consequently, the labour force declined as unemployment grew (chart 4-25). Here a distinction arises between people and place

---

7. In conversation with the author.

Chart 4-30 Massachusetts: Unemployment and Earnings

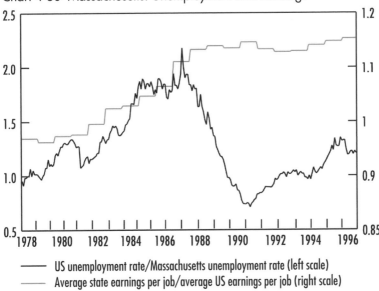

— US unemployment rate/Massachusetts unemployment rate (left scale)
— Average state earnings per job/average US earnings per job (right scale)

Source: U.S. Bureau of Labor Statistics

prosperity. When prosperity in one area declines, people in the United States have historically been open to moving to where jobs and wealth are being created in order to maintain their personal prosperity. This produces good outcomes for the people and for the economy as a whole, because resources are shifted to more productive activities and regions.

But this is only part of the story. In the United States, regions themselves tend to recover their prosperity, though population change will interact with economic conditions. Key elements in restoring "place prosperity" in Massachusetts were wage flexibility and the rise of self-employment and "contingent" workers. Contingent workers work for a company through some contractual arrangement; they are not on its payroll and typically do not receive benefits. "The advantage of these things is that they keep people in jobs," Sum says. "They preserve work-skills." This resolves the paradox, Sum believes, of the difference between the number of jobs lost and the numbers which show up in the Stats USA data-base. Many workers who had lost jobs created their own employment and reported themselves as employed when surveyed. And average pay fell much more than is apparent in payroll data, because of lower remuneration received by self-employed and contingent workers.

All this creates labour-market flexibility. People are willing to work for less, so employers, even in a recession, can afford more workers than they otherwise could. This breaks the fall in employment. With more people working, even if they don't show up in the payroll data, economic activity remains relatively higher. This helps push the economy towards recovery. As the Massachusetts recovery took hold, self-employment and contingent employment fell. Workers moved back to higher-paying, full-time jobs.

Sum believes that, without this labour-market flexibility, the Massachusetts recession would not only have been deeper and unemployment higher, but the recovery would also have been less robust. Without flexible labour costs, firms would have had to further reduce both their work-force and their production. They would have been weaker coming out of the recession. Many people would have fallen out of the work-force for good. Massachusetts would have started down the road towards a Canada-like regional problem – persistently weak economic activity and high unemployment.

Instead, people preserved their job skills, and unemployment has virtually disappeared in Massachusetts. Employment growth has been exceptionally strong since the early 1990s. State per capita GDP, personal income, and average earnings have all begun to rise against the U.S. average. Many folks now think it is the best of times in Massachusetts.

The recovery has been broad based and has not been powered simply by the high-tech sector, as some observers believe. The incomplete recovery of the electronics sector shows this. Because of reduced costs in taxes and wages, a number of sectors have been able to thrive in Massachusetts. But, at the same time, the value of a high-tech, entrepreneurial, independent institution like MIT, both for the regional and national economy, should not be understated:

> If the companies founded by MIT graduates and faculty formed an independent nation, the revenues produced by the companies would make that nation the 24th largest economy in the world. The 4,000 MIT-related companies employ 1.1 million people and have annual world sales of $232 billion. That is roughly equal to a gross domestic product of $116 billion, which is a little less than the GDP of South Africa and more than the GDP of Thailand. (BankBoston 1997, 2)

The recipe for success in Massachusetts was a flexible state cost structure that responded to the downturn, restoring Massachusetts's costs to a level where companies could make profits. That kept companies alive through the downturn and eventually spurred new investment and growth. The key ingredients were a flexible labour market and a government that reacted by reducing taxes and government employment, rather than trying to create make-work projects and a government-managed economic recovery.

MICHIGAN

The stories for Michigan and Massachusetts are broadly similar, so the discussion which follows will be briefer. Michigan became the centre of the "rust belt", a region which had been the midwestern heartland of the United States's industrial might. The rust belt was not just a conceptual idea, but also a raw physical image. Anyone travelling through the industrialized areas of the Midwest, particularly Michigan, would have been struck by the number of deserted, rusting, falling-apart factories that dotted the landscape in the late 1970s and early 1980s. This gave the region a palpable sense of desolation and the apparent promise of a bleak future, as once-vibrant towns and cities became ghost towns and cities, like deserted towns of the Old West. Anyone who has seen the movie *Roger and Me*, a powerful attack on the car industry and government's *laissez-faire* attitude, will have a sense of the stark outlook of the time.

Just as the personal computer decimated the minicomputer sector, the United States's industrial prowess had been crippled – along with confidence in U.S. manufacturing ability – by cheaper, often higher-quality imports from emerging economies. The sudden surge of competition was nowhere more ruinous than in the automobile industry, though other sectors, like machine tools, suffered similar devastation. The external threat was accompanied by another trend. As manufacturing processes became more efficient and automated, fewer workers were needed to manufacture the same amount. Thus, while manufactured goods tended to maintain a fairly constant share of the economy, the number of workers declined – and more and more of those workers lived in Germany or Japan or Korea instead of Michigan or Ohio or Indiana.

From 1977 to 1982, Michigan per capita GDP declined from over 106 per cent of the national average to under 90 per cent (chart 4-31). Similar losses occurred in personal income and average earnings per job (chart 4-32). Job growth was negative for most of the period from mid-1979 to the beginning of 1983 (charts 4-33 and 4-34). The unemployment rate peaked at 16 per cent and was in the double digits for most of the first half of the 1980s, unheard of levels in the United States since the great depression.

But, for the most part, these were the Reagan years, and government was sizing down, not sizing up to help lagging regions. Save for a famous government bail-out of Chrysler, Washington mostly let industries fail and launched no persistent regional-aid programme.[8]

Yet the economies of the rust belt appeared to have had the natural resilience to heal themselves, despite the lack of emer-

---

8. This is not to claim governments did not try to aid U.S. industries in any number of ways. But this was small beer. No rescue efforts of anything like the magnitude common in Canada or Europe were made. Tens of thousands of businesses failed, and thousands of factories were closed.

Chart 4-31 Michigan GSP as a Percentage of USA GSP Per Capita

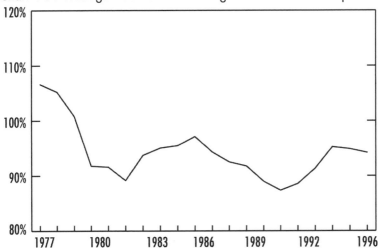

Source: STATS USA

Chart 4-32 Michigan: Relative Personal Income & Earnings

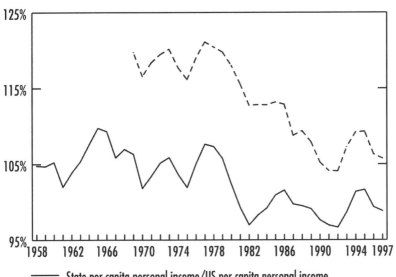

——— State per capita personal income/US per capita personal income

- - - - Average state earnings per job/average US earnings per job

Source: U.S. Bureau of Economic Analysis

Chart 4-33 Michigan Employment and Labour Force

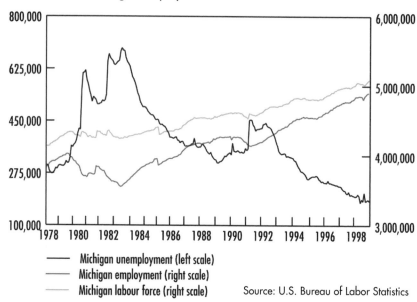

— Michigan unemployment (left scale)
— Michigan employment (right scale)
— Michigan labour force (right scale)

Source: U.S. Bureau of Labor Statistics

Chart 4-34 Michigan Employment Growth

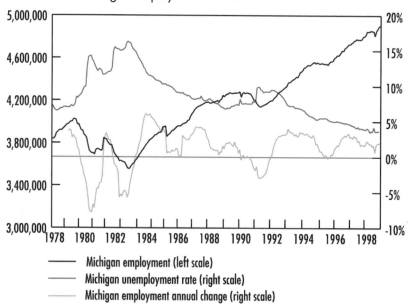

— Michigan employment (left scale)
— Michigan unemployment rate (right scale)
— Michigan employment annual change (right scale)

Source: U.S. Bureau of Labor Statistics

gency government action or even significantly increased protectionism to help the imperiled industries. After 1983, employment growth turned consistently positive, except for a couple of very brief blips and the short economic downturn of the early 1990s. By the beginning of 1987, Michigan's employment exceeded the level of employment that preceded the rust-belt era.

Wages proved flexible throughout the period, something that would have been inhibited by rich regional income-support programmes. Average pay adjusted downwards to levels which generated new employment (chart 4-35). This flexibility reflects two factors. A number of companies negotiated wage concessions with their workers and, often, agreements which allowed them to hire new workers at lower levels of pay. This kept these companies competitive and began to generate new jobs. Loss of high-paying manufacturing jobs also reduced the average pay-level as most displaced workers either accepted lower-paying jobs, left the workforce, remained unemployed, or moved.[9]

State government also reacted with some downsizing, though not particularly dramatically. Personal income taxes initially rose in Michigan as it tried to cope with the downturn, but they have been falling since, albeit with a number of large bumps on the way (chart 4-36). State and local government as a percentage of GDP has continuously declined relative to the national average since the early 1980s. Instead of attempting to generate government employment, state and local government in Michigan significantly reduced employment in the early 1980s. While gov-

---

9. This is an economically efficient process, though many in Canada would argue that, in such cases, efficiency should be moderated by a greater level of public assistance. Personally, I agree with this point of view – that government should help ease transitions. But this becomes a route to long-term economic disaster if government intervention is so large it virtually halts all possible economic adjustment and traps a new generation in declining industries, as has been the case in Cape Breton, for instance, where old, inefficient industries were kept alive with government money and where a rich diet of regionally enhanced UI/EI programmes discouraged people from seeking full-time work, and thereby diminished the ability of businesses to generate such work, because of the wage-cost of competing with UI/EI.

Chart 4-35 Michigan: Unemployment and Earnings

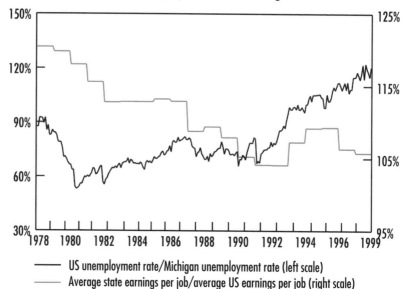

— US unemployment rate/Michigan unemployment rate (left scale)
— Average state earnings per job/average US earnings per job (right scale)

Source: U.S. Bureau of Labor Statistics

Chart 4-36 Michigan State Taxes

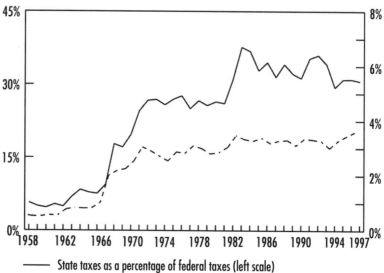

— State taxes as a percentage of federal taxes (left scale)
- - - State taxes as a percentage of personal income (right scale)

Source: STATS USA

Chart 4-37 Michigan: State and Local Government
Employment as a Percentage of Total Employment

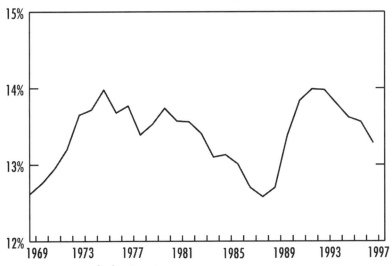

Source: U.S. Bureau of Labor Statistics

ernment employment has been on the rise since the mid-1980s, it has consistently fallen as a percentage of the Michigan work-force for most of the last two decades, with the notable exception of a brief upswing from 1989 to 1991 (chart 4-37).

Although relative per capita GDP, personal income, and average pay have had significant ups and downs since the mid-1980s, each appears to be stabilizing around a new level. It is worth emphasizing that these numbers are all relative to the U.S. average, so a stabilized level means Michigan's per capita GDP, personal income, and average pay are growing at the same healthy rates as those for the U.S. economy as a whole.

In 1991, a new governor, John Engler, was elected. Engler campaigned on getting the government out of the economy and reducing its size. In fact, when he came to power, the state government had been on a hiring binge, finances were weakening, and taxes were again on the rise, as is evident from the charts in this section. Per capita GDP, personal income, and wages were declining against the national average.

By standard Keynesian economics, this was hardly the time to cut government. But that is exactly what Engler did, as a review of the charts which detail government activity will show. Engler argued tax cuts were key to generating jobs. By his own count, he cut taxes 24 times, saving Michigan taxpayers, the administration claims, $11 billion. Whether it was this medicine, the natural resilience of a market-based economy, or a combination of the two, Michigan has exceeded national economic growth through most of the Engler administration.

Through this period, the state has made gains in per capita GDP, personal income, and average wages, though the indicators have widely fluctuated, and it is difficult to say at this point whether the gains are secular. Recent economic news suggests a positive long-term outcome. Michigan's employment growth remains impressive, and its unemployment rate has fallen to the lowest level since the 1960s. It is below the U.S. national average for the first time in generations, and the national unemployment rate has been famously low by international standards for a number of years

Not surprisingly, Gov. Engler's administration credits the increased vigour of the Michigan economy in the 1990s to the administration's efforts to reduce government and cut taxes. Still, Michigan over the last 15 years has exhibited a powerful recovery from what appeared to be a clinically dead state. Few economists in the early 1980s would have predicted the rust-belt economy could ever again be healthy, let alone recover anything like its lost glory. Yet that process is now in place. Although many indicators are lower now than in the 1970s against the national average, because of strong U.S. growth, they have still increased in real terms. Most importantly, unemployment is not just down; it is lower than it was before the regional recession began.

As with Massachusetts, the recovery was not powered by concerted government action but rather the reverse – concerted government restraint though most of the recovery period. Even more important than this was labour-market flexibility. All this opened the potential for profits and, thus, job creation. Many in Michigan now believe this is the best of times.

MAINE

Maine's economy is significantly affected by developments in Massachusetts. The Massachusetts boom of the 1980s spilled over into Maine, inflating the economy and leading to a boom–bust cycle (chart 4-38), particularly in real estate. "A prime piece of shorefront property in the Mount Desert Island area, for example, went for about $10 a front foot in 1960, $100-$200 in the mid-1970s, $500 in 1986, and $1,000 in 1987" (Condon & Barry 1995). These prices made it more expensive for indigenous businesses, as did inflation in wage rates. Government also absorbed increasing resources, and boosted costs directly through taxes and indirectly by putting increased inflationary pressure on the boom. Democrat Joseph Brennan was Maine governor from 1978 to 1986. His eight budgets increased state expenditures between 7.3 and 12.9 per cent each year, pushing up state expenditures from $482 million to $961 million. Brennan's successor, Republican John McKernan, increased expenditures at an even faster rate, peaking in a 19.7 per cent increase in 1989, when state expenditures had jumped to $1.52 billion. In McKernan's first term, state employment increased from 12,492 to 13,710 and pay increased 19 per cent (Condon & Barry 1995, 588-89). Wages also rose dramatically against the national average, though they did with a lag adjust to changes in employment (chart 4-39).

The groundwork for the bust was being laid. Like Michigan and Massachusetts, Maine built larger state and local government during the boom period, but it was much slower in cutting back following the economic downturn than either of those two states, and its reductions were smaller (charts 4-40 and 4-41).

Maine's recovery from the bust of the late 1980s was weaker than Massachusetts's recovery at the same time and Michigan's earlier recovery. Although relative state per capita personal income is now higher than it was in the early 1990s, perhaps in part because of the increasing choice of Maine by wealthy retirees, relative average state earnings are now lower than in the late 1950s (chart 4-42). It is worth noting, however, that this measure is against

Chart 4-38 Maine GSP as a Percentage of USA GSP

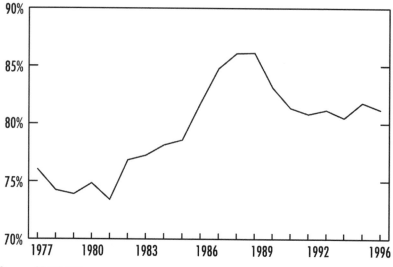

Source: STATS USA

Chart 4-39 Maine: Unemployment and Earnings

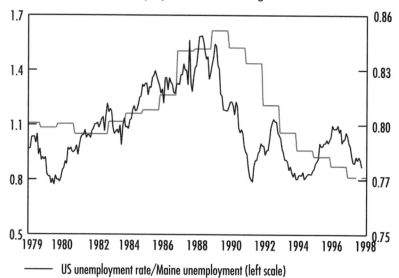

········ US unemployment rate/Maine unemployment (left scale)
———— Average Michigan earnings per job/average US earnings per job (right scale)

Source: U.S. Bureau of Labor Statistics

Chart 4-40 Maine: State Taxes

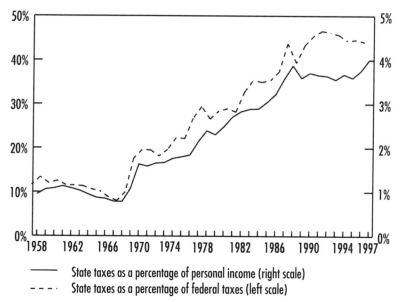

— State taxes as a percentage of personal income (right scale)
- - - · State taxes as a percentage of federal taxes (left scale)

Source: STATS USA

Chart 4-41 Maine: State and Local Employment as a Percentage of Total Employment

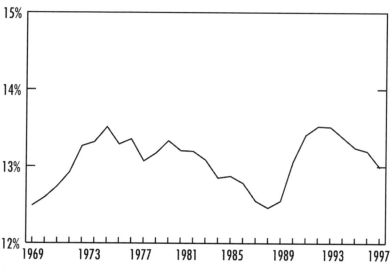

Source: USA BLS

the U.S. average and that, in real terms, Maine's earnings have increased, but not as much as in the national economy. Maine's employment growth was strong during the early part of the 1990s but has weakened since. Nonetheless, unemployment has fallen dramatically because of employment growth, on one hand, and weak labour-force growth, on the other hand (charts 4-43 and 4-44).

The size of Maine's government stands out. Although Maine per capita GDP is just over 80 per cent of the national level, state and local government spend at nearly 90 per cent of the national average (chart 4-45). As noted, the state also has relatively high taxes. In 1994, Maine had the eighth-highest level of state and local taxes in the United States, a level it has fluctuated around for at least the last decade. Maine's state and local employment as a percentage of total employment is also above the national level, but not significantly so. In other words, Maine did not take the same cure as Massachusetts and Michigan – significant reductions in state government and taxes – and has not benefited from as strong an economic turn-around.

A couple of questions about Maine stand out. Maine is showing signs of reducing the size of its government and its tax rates. If it does follow this course, will that be associated with stronger economic growth in the future, as it was in Massachusetts and Michigan? The Maine economy is more resource based than those of other states, and it has doubtlessly been negatively affected by the long-term downward trend in resource prices. But most U.S. states at one time depended on resource-based economies. Will Maine, like these other states, build a modern economy which is not held back by the secular decline in resource prices? Maine's employment growth has experienced both ups and downs since the recovery of the early 1990s, but the unemployment figures conceal very different rates of unemployment within the state, about 2 per cent in the more urban south and about 6 per cent in the predominantly rural north.

Chart 4-42 Maine: Relative Personal Income and Earnings

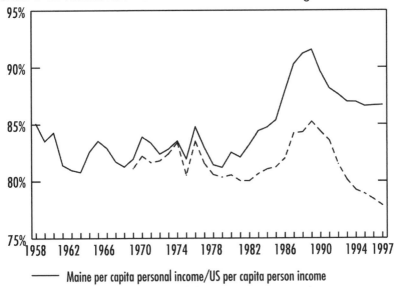

——— Maine per capita personal income/US per capita person income
– – – · Average state earnings per job/average US earnings per job

Source: U.S. Bureau of Economic Analysis

Chart 4-43 Maine: Employment and Labour Force

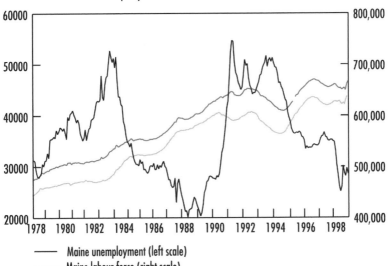

——— Maine unemployment (left scale)
——— Maine labour force (right scale)
——— Maine employment (right scale)   Source: U.S. Bureau of Labor Statistics

Chart 4-44 Maine: Employment Growth

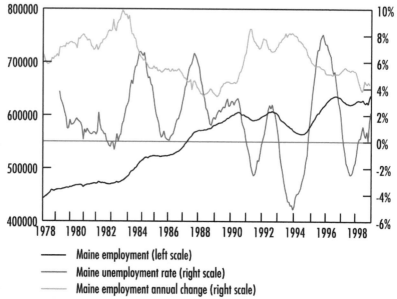

— Maine employment (left scale)
— Maine unemployment rate (right scale)
— Maine employment annual change (right scale)

Source: U.S. Bureau of Labor Statistics

Chart 4-45 Maine: State and Local Government as a Percentage of National Average

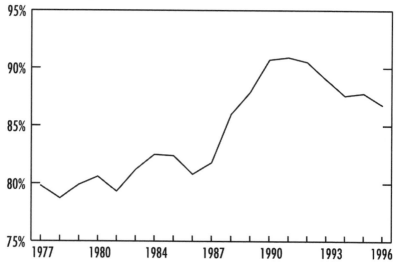

Source: STATS USA

CONCLUSION

All the successful jurisdictions examined have effectively lowered the cost of doing business – and thus increased profit opportunities – in order to spur economic growth and job creation. The two key ingredients examined were cost of labour and cost of government.

Of the five states examined, one, Georgia, has consistently kept government small. It is a right-to-work state, and wages are consistently a notch below the level implied by state per capita GDP. Both the state's economy and wage rates have consistently grown, and Georgia is now much more of a have than a have-not state.

Both Michigan and Massachusetts reacted to a severe economic downturn with reductions in government, though over different time frames. Labour markets proved relatively flexible in both states, as they are through the United States. This allowed wage costs to react to economic developments. Wages decline in a downturn, increasing the cost-attractiveness of the state. This helped local business cope with the downturn and served to draw in new investment.

Two states examined had weak adjustments. Both Louisiana and Maine have relatively large state governments, and both have been bedeviled by resource problems. Louisiana's economy was inflated by resource wealth. The resulting increase in government revenues went to building larger government instead of to reducing costs through lower taxes or providing superior services and government investment. Moreover, by all accounts, much of the money was spent for political, not productive, purposes. As with the Netherlands, resource wealth seems to have done Louisiana more harm than good. Maine also has a relatively large resource dependence which may hold back economic growth, though, as noted, Maine can boast of stronger economic growth than Atlantic Canada or, indeed, Canada as a whole.

Maine and Louisiana – along with a handful of other states, usually high-tax states like West Virginia – are exceptions to the strong force of convergence in the open U.S. economy.

Finally, the U.S. experience should be compared with that of Ireland and the Netherlands. Neither of these nations have labour markets as flexible as those in the United States, though Ireland comes closer than the Netherlands. Still, in both nations, the union movement has a large role in setting wages. Yet the successful Irish and Dutch strategies were remarkably similar to what occurs in the United States, though motivated as much by policy decisions as by the market. While U.S. wages naturally tend down during economic weakness, in the Netherlands and Ireland, government, unions, and business worked together to get the same effect through planning. This led to the Irish and Dutch miracles, though, as noted, whether this corporatist structure can be as flexible in the long term as open markets remains a question. The Dutch and Irish governments also reacted in a similar way to U.S. states seeking stronger growth. Both governments down-sized and worked to reduce taxes. The effort was far more dramatic in Ireland than in the Netherlands, and Irish growth has been stronger.

The dramatic whittling away of regional disparities across the United States has attracted the attention of even strong proponents of regional programmes, who note the phenomena but seem to draw no lessons from it. However, this phenomenon is not universal in the United States. Some high-tax states with an interventionist government and a politicized economy – notably Louisiana and West Virginia – have failed to converge at the average U.S. rate.

Policy-makers should turn their attention to factors that led to the dramatic recoveries in Michigan and Massachusetts and the reasons for the South's long climb from economic obscurity to prosperity. Not only have the Southern states, as a group, been catching up with the rest of the United States, exceeding even the strong overall U.S. rate of economic growth, but the most successful of the Deep South states, Georgia, has exceeded the national level of economic activity. These are stories worth paying attention to.

Conclusion

Policy-makers in lagging economies the world over all too often seek some magic elixir for economic growth. Yet, once cost competitiveness is in place, no magic elixir is required to create jobs and economic growth. They come naturally to competitive market economies, whether in lagging or leading regions. Five hundred years of market economic history makes that clear – people in any market economy live in a society immensely wealthier than did their parents. No other economic structure has even come close to creating the same level of prosperity as market economies.

The world's market economies create hundreds of millions of jobs each generation. Only war, pestilence, or profoundly perverse policies can derail them for anything more than a short period. Modern research shows even the length of Great Depression, though not its onset, was more a policy error – too-tight monetary policy and inflexible wages – than a natural outcome.

Moreover, empirical investigations support theoretical reasons to believe that lagging economies catch up with leading economies. However, this research shows that convergence is not automatic. For convergence to take place, the lagging jurisdiction requires the essentials of a market economy: markets, property rights, the rule of law, and stable institutions. An educated populace, or at least one that puts an emphasis on improving education levels, is also essential. Outside this convergence club, the gap between market and non-market economies is growing. Or, put another way, the gap between rich and poor is growing.

Among market economies – whether in Europe, the United States, or Japan – convergence shows up strongly. As we'll see in *Retreat from Growth*, the sequel to this book, convergence is far weaker in Canada, although Canada launched perhaps the world's most heroic regional wealth-transfer and development programme.

Convergence is partly due to the spread of productive ideas and methods. But costs and the profit motive also play a central role. An under-invested economy creates profit opportunities. A key mechanism here is the idea of labour/capital ratio. When labour is abundant relative to capital – as is the case in lagging economies – labour costs should be relatively low. Potential returns, profits, on the scarce resource, capital, should be relatively high. The profit motive attracts capital and creates jobs and economic growth. This can be derailed by distortions in the economy that either artificially inflate wages or attack the return to capital. This not only stymies investment and economic growth, it also stunts the potential for wage growth over the longer term.

TWO-FOLD PURPOSE

This concluding chapter is not designed solely to provide a conceptual overview of and conclusion to the material found in this book. It is also meant to provide a forward glance to *Retreat from Growth*, which focuses on another type of economic-development strategy – one of heroic government intervention and regional wealth transfers designed to spark growth. The case study is Atlantic Canada, which has received immense wealth transfers from the central government and experimented with an unusual number of differing approaches to government-directed development.

The nations and U.S. states studied in this volume took a very different approach. Not only did they reduce intervention in the economy – for example, moving away from subsidies in Ireland and the Netherlands – they explicitly aimed to reduce costs to spur economic activity.

This approach marks economies which succeed in overcoming backwardness, whether in times past – for example, the United States when it was a lagging economy – or currently, as can be seen in transition of the successful Eastern European economies. In the latter case, the key policy challenge was establishing the institutions needed for democracy and a market economy. Once these attributes were in place in former Soviet-bloc countries, low costs came nearly automatically because of the low standard of living and low expectations of the people under the Communist regimes that had ruled these nations. Now, new prosperity is being established in nations like Hungary, the Czech Republic, and Poland. Incomes and wages are rising.

In Ireland and the Netherlands, three key costs – taxes, government, and wages – could either be controlled or influenced by policy-makers. Both nations directly tackled the first of these costs. Ireland undertook huge tax cuts in the late 1980s. The Netherlands first tried to control taxes in the early 1980s, but tax cuts were relatively low. The Netherlands has more aggressively tackled tax levels in recent years.

Government doesn't create costs solely through taxes. High government debts and deficits increase costs through the uncertainty related to inflation, concerns about future tax increases needed to pay down the debt, and increased borrowing costs which suppress private-sector investment. Ireland and the Netherlands got these costs under control by slashing the deficit and, more slowly, whittling away the debt relative to GDP. Heavy-handed government regulation also creates costs. Ireland had never developed an over-regulated economy. The Dutch are moving aggressively to eliminate unnecessary regulation in their economy.[1]

Government can also increase costs in an economy through programme spending. The impact is indirect. Costs are introduced by distortions in the economy. The most prevalent are labour-market distortions caused by government supports that discourage people from working. The Netherlands is reforming its perverse disability system, while the Irish are attempting to tackle long-term unemployment through changes to the unemployment system and tax relief for low-wage workers. As well, when government expands, high public-sector employment and wages compete against private-sector employers.

Wage levels are essential to both the Irish and Dutch stories. In both nations, the corporatist actors in the economy – unions, busi-

---

1. On the subject of the most fruitful approach to government regulation, see a forthcoming AIMS study of regulation, by Brian Flemming.

ness, and government – worked together to restore wage competitiveness. Yet real wages have actually risen more rapidly under a union strategy of wage moderation than they did under a regime of aggressive union bargaining.

All the U.S. states examined in this volume that succeeded in sparking strong economic growth either moved to cut taxes and government size, or consistently kept taxes low and government small. Policy-makers in both Michigan and Massachusetts believed high state taxes had slowed state growth and contributed to their regional recession. Both states cut taxes, spending, and government employment, despite high levels of unemployment by U.S. standards. The private sector responded: it created hundreds of thousands of jobs more than government had cut. Both states boast unemployment rates below five per cent. Georgia has long maintained small government and low taxes, and this helped transform Georgia from a lagging state to a leading state.

U.S. policy-makers do not have corporatist tools for influencing wage levels, but the flexible U.S. labour market accomplished the same end achieved in Ireland and the Netherlands – competitive wage levels appropriate to current economic conditions.

INTERVENTIONIST POLICIES

In some jurisdictions, policy-makers seem largely to ignore the fact that costs are key to economic growth and the implications of this fact – for example, the impact of taxes on creating jobs and wealth. Instead, they attempt a more direct approach to economic development, either through government enterprise or through government's selection of certain companies or sectors for favoured treatment through government contracts, subsidies, or special tax concessions. The impact of such interventionist policy will be more extensively examined *Retreat from Growth*, but for now it is important to make the contrast between this interventionist approach and the market-oriented cost approach.

In some jurisdictions, like Atlantic Canada, interventionist policies still dominate, despite a long record of failure. In part, this is political. Policy-makers gain more power from interventionist policies and can take credit for direct job creation or job preservation. But, as will be seen in the next volume, such policies create hidden losers. The high taxes needed to support such policies raise taxes for all businesses, except those receiving the subsidies. Unsubsidized businesses face other increased costs. They have to compete with subsidized businesses for resources, most notably labour. These extra costs will discourage business formation, slow growth among unsubsidized businesses, and increase the rate of failure. But these are unseen costs – businesses that either haven't formed or grown as much as they would have, or business failures attributed not to policy but to general economic conditions. Thus, policy-makers can take credit for the results of direct intervention while side-stepping blame for the negative consequences created elsewhere in the economy.

The argument for government intervention is based on the idea of market failure. According to this view, the cost structure of an economy is of small relevance. Instead, market failures, particularly in providing capital to lagging and peripheral regions, mean that investors will ignore, or be ignorant of, profit-making opportunities. Thus, since a low-cost structure will do little to spur development and attract investment, and since lagging regions themselves don't have the capital for investment, richer governments must sponsor regional-development programmes that transfer wealth to the lagging region. This gives government the means for direct intervention in the economy, enabling it to solve this market failure either by investing itself or by bribing private investors into the lagging region through subsidies.

This view is obviously wrong. It is directly contradicted by the evidence of convergence between lagging economies with leading economies, whether or not regional programmes are in place. In this book, the contradiction can be seen in the experience of Ireland and the American Deep South. Both were long-time lagging regions. Both were on the periphery of economic activity. Both have experienced strong convergence despite either the lack of regional programmes, for the Deep South, or the presence of fairly weak regional programmes, in the case of Ireland. Both are now outperforming some leading economies at the centre of economic activity. More surprisingly, as discussed in *Retreat from Growth: Atlantic Canada and the Negative Sum Economy* (McMahon 2000), the lagging region with perhaps the world's most heroic regional-development programme – Atlantic Canada – has underperformed the convergence effect and underperformed lagging regions which receive little or no outside government help.

High government spending and interventionist policies would not present a problem if government activity could itself create self-sustaining jobs, jobs that did not require continuing subsidies that are, in effect, paid for by other sectors of the economy, weakening those self-sustaining sectors.

But government's record in this area has been dismal. One often-noted problem has been government's inability to pick winners with future economic potential. Government's track record gives overwhelming evidence of this failure. But less noted is government's bias towards picking losers, the declining industries of yesterday. These come with a ready-made lobby of voters and businesses who can provide political benefits in exchange for state aid.

Government intervention also politicizes the economy, a recipe for the misallocation of resources. Powerful bureaucrats and politicians are able to direct resources to benefit politically important groups and interests, rather than to their most productive uses. This is a key reason why heroic economic-development efforts have failed to generate sustainable prosperity, and one of the reasons such efforts persist in the face of powerful evidence of their ineffectiveness and wastefulness. They continue to provide political benefits.

These programmes also change incentives in the economy. When companies' profits are maintained by government contracts and subsidies – say, the point at which government spending equals more than 50 per cent of GDP – business incentives move away from producing goods and services people want to buy. Instead, they move towards rent-seeking – that is, currying favour with politicians and bureaucrats in order to obtain government supports and contracts. This can have a devastating impact on the business sector, something we'll examine in *Retreat from Growth*. Taxes also have to be high enough to pay for intervention. Aside from directly increasing the costs of government, this leads to further misallocation of resources. Profitable businesses, which pay taxes and generate jobs without cost to government, find their tax dollars going to less-successful competitors and other activities which are all too often selected to receive government largesse in the form of subsidies or preferential contracts because of their political power.

However, one of the most serious and most over-looked problems with intervention is its indirect impact on costs. Government spending and subsidies for government-selected private-sector investment bid up the price of scarce resources, discouraging investment not supported by government. Since government investment, and its ability to pick winners, has a poor track record, the cost-inflated suppression of other investment is likely to more than offset whatever benefits government-aided investment provides.

The strategy of government-directed regional economic development is often supported by wealth transfers to lagging regions. The key question, of course, is how such transfers are typically used. If these transfers primarily go to consumption, rather than investment, then any sort of economic analysis indicates this will result in increased costs in the economy. Wealth transfers, if used for consumption, bid up the costs of scarce resources in the economy. This makes investment more expensive, and suppresses investment that would have taken place in the absence of wealth transfers. That can only damage self-sustaining development. The evidence supports such analyses. Although some jurisdictions (e.g., Ireland) carefully direct outside help to productive investment, wealth transfers, whether in the form of foreign aid or regional aid – say, in the case of Atlantic Canada – predominantly inflate consumption at the cost of investment. This evidence will be reviewed in *Retreat from Growth* (McMahon 2000).

WAGES

Although government-directed economic development has consistently failed, there remains resistance to the idea of holding down costs, particularly labour costs. This is viewed as a demeaning approach that is unfair to working people. It only creates a "race to the bottom", critics say, which locks the economy in competition with other low-wage, low-cost jurisdictions. Yet, as numbers we have examined conclusively show, the exact opposite is the case. The low-cost, market-oriented approach leads ultimately to higher wages, because of increased investment and skill acquisition, leading to higher productivity.

Competitive wages result in solid profits. The opportunity to make profits draws in investment. Consequent increases in physical capital and skills – human capital – through increased training and through learning-by-doing drive up the value of labour by increasing productivity. Employers can afford to pay more and still maintain relatively low wage costs in relation to the productivity of labour. Thus, the company can continue to be profitable while increasing pay. Provided wage increases do not squeeze out profits, this begins a virtuous circle. Profits continue to attract investment. Investment continues to increase the value of labour. This permits another round of wage increases while profits remain healthy, and so the virtuous circle continues to turn.

But if wages rise to the point where profits are squeezed out, investment inevitably declines, unemployment rises, and the value of labour stagnates. The value of labour stagnates because of low investment and reduced opportunities to improve skills. This creates a vicious circle. Wages squeeze out profits. Investment declines. Skills erode. The value of labour stagnants or declines. Real wages decline. Worker militancy is likely to increase in the face of weak or negative wage growth. Aggressive bargaining continues to wreck profits, investment continues to decline, as do real wages, regardless of the nominal settlement, and so the vicious circle continues to turn.

This means that workers who practise wage moderation to boost profits will actually see greater wage increases over the long term than workers who aggressively bargain for the highest possible wage in any given year. In other words, the race to the bottom is actually a climb to the top. This rather counter-intuitive proposition is strongly borne out by the experience of the Netherlands and Ireland, where a period of aggressive wage bargaining was followed by a strategy of wage moderation. Real wages grew more strongly and consistently under wage moderation than under aggressive bargaining, which often led to declines in real wages, even while nominal wages were increasing. In the United States, too, where unions are relatively weak, real wages have grown much more strongly than in Canada, where unions are relatively strong and typically seek the highest possible settlement for any given contract.

Georgia may be considered a low-wage state, but wages in Georgia are higher than in Canada. This is because the capital attracted to Georgia and the skills of the work-force permit higher levels of pay while still allowing investors to reap substantial profits.

TAXES

Just as there is resistance to wage moderation as a tool of development, many commentators object to reducing taxes. This, too, they claim, is a race to the bottom, in this case in government services. But it is important to understand that taxes may be considered the cost of government services, so whether the cost is high or low depends on the value of the goods and services provided in return. Fifteen thousand dollars may be a high cost for a 10-year-old wreck, but it's a low cost for a new Mercedes. Thus, one jurisdiction with a moderate tax regime may provide excellent value for money while another, which inefficiently spends government resources, should properly be considered a high-cost area.

The real question about taxes concerns what might be called their "net" cost – the amount of taxes paid, along with some calculation of the both the positives and negatives provided in return for taxes. A low-tax jurisdiction might be a high *net-cost* tax jurisdiction if the government fritters away tax dollars. A moderate-tax jurisdiction, on the other hand, might be a low *net-cost* tax jurisdiction if large benefits are provided efficiently. Thus, the idea of low costs, including low taxes, does not imply a vanishingly small government. For example, a jurisdiction does not have to have taxes as low as those in Georgia to succeed, but it does need to spend its tax revenues wisely to succeed.

When governments collect money in taxes and spend them on services that genuinely benefit the population, they very often also reduce costs for businesses. This is not to argue that all government policies should be directed at reducing costs. Many factors motivate government policy, but good policy tends not only to make a jurisdiction a better place to live, but also to make it a better place to do business. For example, both education and health care are essential to citizens and to business. An educated populace reduces training and education costs for business. An efficient government-provided medical-care system provides a better life for a nation's citizens and better workers for companies. It saves on the cost of providing private health care. So, properly run, Medicare in Canada, for example, is a competitive advantage.

Moreover, in the same way that competitive wages do not imply a race to the bottom in wages, competitive taxes do not imply a race to the lowest-possible tax revenue. In fact, once again, the real case is quite the reverse. Just as competitive wages open the door to sustainable real wage increases, competitive taxes help boost sustainable economic activity which raises the tax take. Typically, one or two years after a significant tax cut, tax revenues are higher than prior to the cut. They may be lower as a percentage of GDP, but they are higher in real terms because GDP growth has been strong.

But problems arise when taxes are used for policies that focus large benefits on small numbers of people. For example, an efficient transportation structure to important markets is essential for growth. If it suffers from underinvestment while little-used roads in politically important constituencies are well tended, and if contracts are awarded based on patronage not efficiency, then the whole economy suffers. Everyone pays higher taxes for services that benefit primarily the politically connected. This same criticism may be levelled at most economic-development efforts, which, in the end, only transfer wealth from self-sustaining activities to government-selected activities, benefiting the set of owners and workers in the selected activities, while harming other businesses and workers.

Bad policy can increase costs both directly through taxes and indirectly through distortions in the market-place. For example, economic growth and job creation would be stifled by a disability system so generous and easy to tap into that people become unwilling to work. This happened in the Netherlands. It creates huge costs. Business has to compete with government – with their own tax dollars – to attract workers. That drives up labour costs, thwarts expansion plans, and suppresses investment. Why invest and create jobs if the company cannot get anyone to fill them at wages the company can afford to pay?

Thus, costs are raised both directly, through paying taxes, and indirectly, through the effect of the programmes funded by these higher taxes. The same problem which afflicted the Dutch economy because of its disability system would be created by an unemployment-insurance system so generous people shun work to collect unemployment-insurance payments. This happened in Atlantic Canada, as is examined in *Retreat from Growth*. At times, nearly twice as many collected unemployment as were unemployed. This created labour shortages throughout the region and thwarted growth because businesses either couldn't find workers or had to bid against the unemployment system to obtain workers, thus increasing costs and stunting investment. Recent research shows that many of recipients of unemployment benefits in Atlantic Canada will refuse work even if government offers to subsidize wages. This immobilizes large parts of the work-force and profoundly damages economic opportunity.

A Challenge for Policy-makers

The idea of cost in an economy is relatively straightforward. In corporatist economies, policy-makers have tools to directly affect wage rates, taxes, and other government-related costs. In the North American setting, policy-makers can directly affect taxes and other government costs. Wage rates can only be influenced indirectly by policy – for example, labour-market regulation, unionization laws, and social-support programmes that may compete with employers for workers.

The question of whether wages are competitive does not depend solely on the wage level. The key point is the value being returned for labour. Thus, in Ireland and the Netherlands a strategy of wage moderation – by leading to increased investment and economic activity – sparked a long-term rise in real wages. Similarly, the question of whether a jurisdiction has a high-cost or a low-cost government is not simply a matter of the level of taxation. Rather, it is the tax level, and other costs related to government, in relation to the value of the services government is providing that determines the real cost to the economy.

These complications motivate this book's effort to examine a wide range of policies in an equally wide range of economies that had to address a number of differing economic problems. Policy-makers in the successful economies examined adopted the same fundamental strategy, that of making their economy more competitive by reducing costs.

Consideration of cost in an economy to spark growth is not a matter of ideology, though some view it that way. This book has examined success stories from the soft-left milieu of the Netherlands to the ideologically hard-to-classify Ireland. We've also looked at success stories in the more market-oriented United States.

Yet, despite their differences, all these areas have something in common. They all experienced hard times, either historically, like Ireland and the southern United States, or from set-backs like those in the Netherlands, Michigan, and Massachusetts. They all tackled costs in their economy. And now they're all growing strongly

– generating new wealth, and more and better-paying jobs.
These results contrast sharply with those in other lagging economies – most notably, Atlantic Canada – that initiated heroic
efforts to encourage economic growth, but through very different
policies. These polices focused on government-directed economic
growth but paid little attention to the costs in the economy. Atlantic Canada is characterized by immense wealth transfers from more
prosperous regions of the nation; very large government, even by
European standards; and large economic-development programmes. As we shall see, such policies often inflated costs and
thus weakened overall economic growth. One clear fact stands
out: Atlantic Canada's economy has underperformed other lagging regions, whether in Europe, Japan, or the United States. This
is a remarkable result, given the effort to boost regional development in Atlantic Canada. We'll look at this more closely in *Retreat
from Growth.*

Appendix

The Corporatist Economy

Some readers will object to the phrase "corporatist economy", since markets are strong in these economies, and corporatist entities hardly have full control overriding market signals. But economies don't come in pure forms and the corporatist label is useful in distinguishing these economies from even more market-oriented economies, such as in the United States, where corporatist bodies have little or no influence over market signals.

Of course, there are other types of economies. The state-managed economy, under many different guises, has never experienced anything than long-term failure, sometimes preceded by short-term success. A less extreme form of state-managed economy is one where government agencies attempt to get around markets, either by direct state investment or through subsidies to selected businesses which agree to make the investments the state wants. Thus, state activity either supplements or replaces the profit motive. To some extent, this characterizes economic policy in Atlantic Canada, the subject of *Retreat from Growth: Atlantic Canada and the Negative Sum Economy* (McMahon 2000).

References

Ady, Robert M. 1997. "Discussion [of Fisher (1997)]." *New England Economic Review* (March/April): 77-82.

Alesina, A., and R. Perotti. 1995. "Fiscal Adjustment: Fiscal Expansions and Adjustments in OECD Countries." *Economic Policy: A European Forum 21*: 205-249.

Arrow, Kenneth J. 1997. "Economic Growth Policy for a Small Country." In Alan W. Gray (ed.), *International Perspectives on the Irish Economy*, 1-8. Dublin: Indecon Economic Consultants.

Baker, Terry. 1997. *The Roots of Irish Growth.* Dublin: Economic and Social Research Institute.

BankBoston. 1997. *MIT: The Impact of Innovation.* Boston: BankBoston.

Barro, Robert, and Xavier Sala-i-Martin. 1995. *Economic Growth.* New York: McGraw-Hill.

Barry, F., and M. B. Devereux. 1995. "The 'Expansionary Fiscal Contraction' Hypothesis: A Neo-Keynesian Analysis." *Oxford Economic Papers 47*: 241-264.

Bartik, Timothy J. 1997. "Discussion [of Wasylenko (1997)]." *New England Economic Review* (March/April): 67-71.

Baumol, William J. 1994. "Multivariate Growth Patterns: Contagion and Common Forces as Possible Sources of Convergence." In William J. Baumol, Richard R. Nelson, and Edward N. Wolff (eds.), *Convergence of Productivity: Cross-national Studies and Historical Evidence.* 62-85. New York: Oxford University Press.

Baumol, William J., Richard R. Nelson, and Edward N. Wolff (eds.). *1994.Convergence of Productivity: Cross-national Studies and Historical Evidence.* New York: Oxford University Press.

de Búrca, Seán. 1997. "Core-peripheral Relationships as the Nexus in World Trade Trends." In Brian Fynes and Sean Ennis (eds.), *Competing From the Periphery: Core Issues in International Business.* 17-45. Dublin: Oak Tree Press.

Burda, Michael C. 1997. "Persistently High Irish Unemployment: A Comparison with the U.K." In Alan W. Gray (ed.), *International Perspectives on the Irish Economy.* 85-111. Dublin: Indecon Economic Consultants.

Burnside, Craig, and David Dollar. 1998. *Aid, the Incentive Regime, and Poverty Reduction.* Policy Research Working Papers No. 1937. Washington:World Bank, Development Research Group.

Cellucci, Argeo Paul. 1997. Governor's Report on The Commonwealth of Massachusetts. Boston: The Commonwealth.

Condon, Richard H., and William David Barry. 1995. "The Tides of Change, 1967-1988." In Richard W.Judd, Edwin A. Churchill, and Joel W.Eastman (eds.), *Maine: The Pine Tree State from Prehistory to the Present.* 554-85. Orono: University of Maine Press.

Corporation for Enterprise Development (CFED). 1996. The 1996 Development Report Card for the States: Economic Benchmarks for State and Corporate Decision-makers. Washington: The Corporation.

CPB (Netherlands Bureau for Economic Policy Analysis). 1997. Challenging Neighbours: Rethinking German and Dutch Economic Institutions. Berlin: Springer.

de la Fuente, Angel, and Xavier Vives. 1997. "The Sources of Irish Growth." In Alan W. Gray (ed.), *International Perspectives on the Irish Economy.* 112-134. Dublin: Indecon Economic Consultants.

Dollar, David, and Lant Pritchett. 1998. *Assessing Aid: A World Bank Policy Research Report.* New York: Oxford University Press.

DRI Canada, APEC, and Canmac Economics Ltd. 1994. *Atlantic Canada: Facing the Challenge of Change: A Study of the Atlantic Economy.* Moncton, N.B.: Atlantic Canada Opportunities Agency.

Dutch Economic Indicators, December 1998: Statistics Netherlands: www.cbs.nl/en/figures/economic-indicators/index.htm

Economic and Social Research Institute (ESRI). 1997a. Medium
Term Review: 1997-2003. (prepared by David Duffy, John
Fitzgerald, Ide Kearney, and Fergal Shortall.) Dublin: The In-
stitute.

———. 1997b. EU Structural Funds in Ireland: A Mid-Term Evaluation of the CSF 1994-99. Patrick Honohan (ed.). Dublin: The
Institute.

Fisher, Ronald C. 1997. "The Effects of State and Local Public
Services on Economic Development." *New England Economic
Review* (March/April): 53-82.

Flynn, Patricia M., Bennett Harrison, William F. Cox, Peter D.
Enrich, and Robert D. Ebel. 1997. "Policy Implications. A Panel
Discussion," in Federal Reserve Bank of Boston, *New England
Economic Review.* march/April. 1997.

Haughton, Jonathan. 1995. "The Historical Background." In J. W.
O'Hagan (ed.), *The Economy of Ireland: Policy and Performance of
a Small European Country.* 1-48. Dublin: Gill & Macmillan.

Higgins, Benjamin, and Donald Savoie. 1995. *Regional Development Theories and Their Application.* New Brunswick, NJ: Transaction Publishers.

Holmes, Thomas J. 1996. *The Effect of State Policies on the Location
of Industry: Evidence from State Borders.* Research Department
Staff Report 205. Minneapolis, MN: Federal Reserve Bank of
Minneapolis.

Industrial Development Agency (IDA) Ireland. 1995. (IDA) Ireland: Annual Report 1994. Dublin: The Agency.

Irish Independent. 20 June 1998. Dublin.6

King, R. G., and S. Rebelo. 1990. "Public Policy and Economic
Growth: Developing Neoclassical Implications." *Journal of
Political Economy* 98 (5 pt.2): S126-S150.

Klaver, Jan A. M. 1997. "The Dutch Economy: From Straggler to Runner-up."Address to the conference of the Julius Raab Foundation on strategies for smaller countries in global competition, Vienna.

Krugman, Paul R. 1997. "Good News from Ireland: A Geographical Perspective." In Alan W. Gray (ed.), *International Perspectives on the Irish Economy.* 38-53. Dublin: Indecon Economic Consultants.

Lane, Philip R. 1995. "Government Intervention." In J. W. O'Hagan (ed.), *The Economy of Ireland: Policy and Performance of a Small European Country.* 104-126. Dublin: Gill & Macmillan.

Leddin, Anthony, and Jim O'Leary. 1995. "Fiscal, Monetary and Exchange Rate Policy." In J. W. O'Hagan (ed.), *The Economy of Ireland: Policy and Performance of a Small European Country.* 159-195. Dublin: Gill & Macmillan.

Massachusetts Taxpayers Foundation. 1997. Interstate Tax comparisons: Where does Massachusetts Stand? Boston: The Foundation.

McMahon, Fred. 2000. *Retreat from Growth: Atlantic Canada and the Negative Sum Economy.* Halifax, N.S.: Atlantic Institute for Market Studies.

National Economic and Social Council (NESC). 1996. *Strategy into the 21ˢᵗ Century.* Dublin: The Council.

Netherlands. 1997. Ministry of Economic Affairs. 1997. *Benchmarking the Netherlands: Prepared for the Future?* The Hague: The Ministery.

Nickell, Steve, and Jan van Ours. 1999. *The Netherlands and the United Kingdom: A European Unemployment Miracle.* Ottawa: Centre for the Study of Living Standards (CSLS) Conference on the Structural Aspects of Unemployment in Canada.

OECD 1998a OECS Economic Surveys, 1998: Netherlands, Paris: OECD

OECD. 1997a. OECD Economic Surveys, 1996-97: Ireland. Paris: OECD.

OECD 1997b. OECD Main Economic Indicators: Historical Statistics, 1960-1996. CD-ROM. Paris: OECD.

Ó Gráda, Cormac. 1997. *A Rocky Road: The Irish Economy since the 1920s.* Manchester: Manchester University Press.

O'Malley, Eoin. 1998. "The Revival of Irish Indigenous Industry 1987-1997." In Economic and Social Research Institute (ESRI). "Quarterly Economic Commentary: april 1998," prepared by T.J. Baker, David Duffy, and Fergal Shortall, Dublin.

O'Sullivan, Mary. 1995. "Manufacturing and Global Competition." In J. W.O'Hagan (ed.), *The Economy of Ireland: Policy and Performance of a Small European Country.* 363-396. Dublin: Gill & Macmillan.

Sachs, Jeffrey D. 1997. "Ireland's Growth Strategy: Lessons for Economic Development." In Alan W. Gray (ed.), *International Perspectives on the Irish Economy.* 54-63. Dublin: Indecon Economic Consultants.

Sachs, Jeffrey D., and Andrew Warner. 1995. "Economic Reform and the Process of Global Integration." *Brookings Papers in Economic Activity* 1: 1995: 1-118.

SER (Social and Economic Council of the Netherlands; Sociaal-Economische Raade). 1998. "Summary of SER Advisory Report Social-economic Policy 1998-2002." The Hague: The Council.

Stanford, Jim. 1999. *Paper Boom: Why Real Prosperity Requires a New Approach to Canada's Economy.* Toronto: Lorimer.

Tannenwald, Robert. 1997. "State Regulatory Policy and Economic Development." *New England Economic Review* (March/April): 83-107.

Tansey, Paul. 1998. *Ireland at Work: Economic Growth and the Labour Market, 1987-1997.* Dublin: Oak Tree Press.

Tax Foundation. 1997. *Facts and Figures on Government Finance, 31st ed.* Patrick Fleennor (ed.) Washington: Tax Foundation, Inc.

Toft, Graham. 1995. "Industrial Development in the New

Economy." *Journal of Applied Manufacturing Systems* 8(1): Winter 1995-96. Minnesota: St. Thomas Technology Press: 5-10.

van Ark, Bart, and Jakob de Haan. 1997. *The Delta-Model Revisited: Recent Trends in the Structrural Performance of the Dutch Economy.* Research Memorandum GD-38. Groningen: University of Groningen, Groningen Growth and Development Centre.

van Empel, Frank. 1997. *The Dutch Model: The Power of Consultation in the Netherlands.* The Hague: The Labour Foundation (STAR--Stichting van de Arbeid).

Visser, Jelle, and Anton Hemerijck. 1997. *"A Dutch Miracle": Job Growth, Welfare Reform and Corporatism in the Netherlands.* Amsterdam: Amsterdam University Press.

VNO-NCW (Confederation of Netherlands Industry and Employers). 1997a. *The Dutch Economy: Country Profile, Recent Developments and Prospects.* The Hague: The Confederation.

–––. 1997b. *The Dutch Economy: From Morass to Successful Polder Model?* The Hague: The Confederation.

Wasylenko, Michael. 1997. "Taxation and Economic Development: The State of Economic Literature." *New England Economic Review* (March/April): 37-52.

Weinstein, Bernard, and Robert Firestine. 1978. *Regional Growth and Decline in the United States: The Rise of the Sunbelt and the Decline of the Northeast.* New York: Praeger.

Wright, Gavin. 1986. *Old South, New South: Revolutions in the Southern Economy since the Civil War.* Baton Rouge: Louisiana State University Press.

World Bank. 1997. World Development Indicators: 1997. CD-ROM. Washington: World Bank.

Index

subsidies; Ireland, 89, 90, 92;
   Atlantic Canada, 90; Georgia,
   160
Sum, Andy, 182, 183
Tannewald, Robert, 41
Tansey, Paul, 93
tax reductions, 13, 25; Ireland, 41,
   69;
taxes and public services, 30-38,
   64, 209-210; the Netherlands,
   122-123; problem of measurement, 32; social programmes,
   106; transportation, 32, 35;
   state, 152
Toft, Graham, 159
unions, 40; Ireland, 39, 42; the
   Netherlands, 39, 42, 101-2,
   104; United States, 39
United States, the; labour market,
   142; military spending, 146,
   147; regional development
   programmes, 141, 142; unions,
   142-143; see also Georgia,
   Louisiana, Maine, Massachusetts, Michigan
van Agt, Andries, 105-106
van Empel, Frank, 137-138
Vives, Xavier, 79, 80
wage increases, 26, 70
Wassenaar agreement, 112-115,
   131
Wasylenko, 33, 36
Weinstein, Bernard, Firestine,
   Robert, 146, 147, 151, 160
World Bank, 34
Wright, Gavin, 146, 154, 156

 FRED MCMAHON is a founding member of the Atlantic Institute for Market Studies (AIMS) and the institute's Senior Policy Analyst. He is the author of the Institute's first book, *Looking the Gift Horse in the Mouth: The Impact of Federal Transfers on Atlantic Canada*, which won the US$10,000 Sir Antony Fisher International Memorial Award for advancing public policy debate. He has prepared numerous research reports for the institute; his articles have appeared in many publications including the *National Post* and the *Globe and Mail*; and his column runs in several Atlantic Canadian newspapers. Prior to joining AIMS, he was Economics Editor with the Bank of Canada where he edited the Bank's flagship publication, *The Bank of Canada Review*. He has also been a researcher with the U.S. Policy Studies Group at Dalhousie University and an economics journalist or editor with the *Financial Post*, the Montreal *Daily News* and the *Halifax Herald*. He has an MA in economics from McGill University. Since completing this book, he has joined the Consumer Policy Institute in Toronto as Policy Director.